The Alliance of Independent Authors

The Alliance of Independent Authors
is a global non-profit association for self publishing writers.

Website: allianceindependentauthors.org
Blog: selfpublishingadvice.org

Opening Up To Indie Authors

Debbie Young & Dan Holloway
Series editor: Orna Ross

An Alliance of Independent Authors' Guide
www.allianceindependentauthors.org

Opening Up To Indie Authors.
Font Publications London UK.

ISBN EBOOK: 978-1-909888-14-2
ISBN PRINT: 987-1-909888-13-5
ISBN AUDIOBOOK: 978-1-909888-15-9

Category: Writing, Publishing

Introduction:
Launch Speech at
The London Book Fair 2014

by Orna Ross
Director of The Alliance of Independent Authors (ALLi)

You've written a book, hired a crack editor, encased it in a jacket that is a work of art and formatted the interior with lustrous font and arresting headings. You've put it out there and lo! you've gained some readers. A fantastic achievement.

Now you'd like your book in a bookstore or library. You'd like to attend one of the literary events that are mushrooming up near you. You'd like to join the appropriate association for your genre. Except you can't.

According to the people running the shop or library or festival or association, you're not *really* published. Even if you sell more books, and have more great reviews than some of the writers they're headlining, you fail to qualify.

This situation grew out of historical circumstances but it's wrong. It's depriving readers of great books and literary organisations of new, dynamic input from some of the most forward-thinking and hard-working authors.

We need change.

This guidebook is part of a campaign that aims to foster that change: ALLi's *Open Up To Indie Authors* campaign (found on Twitter and other places online with the hashtag #PublishingOpenUp).

Publishing is changing on every front, and rapidly. Today, half or more of the books on Amazon and other ebook bestseller lists are self-published. ALLi has many members who have sold more than 100,000 copies of their books; some who have sold in their millions. Many more are producing work of outstanding literary merit. And corporate publishers and agents are watching all this and scouting for successful self-published authors, hoping to woo them with a trade publishing contract.

These changes have yet to be reflected throughout the literary infrastructure of libraries, reviews, bookstores, festivals and prizes. This book, and the associated campaign, hopes to change that.

Our organisation represents self-publishers all over the world and this book is for them — but also for the book fairs and conferences, award bodies and libraries, festival and event organisers, retailers and reviewers who now need to accommodate them in their work.

If you're someone who acts as a conduit between writer and reader, we're calling on you to to open up. Open up to what? To the most exciting and expansive movement in the books business for centuries: author publishing.

And if you're a self-published writer, we're calling on you to understand that often it isn't an anti-indie conspiracy that sees you out in the cold but various constraints that the industry and its offshoots must operate within. And also to know that there are many things you can do to help your cause.

You will find them all within.

Author-Publishing

At ALLi, independent authors come in many guises but are united by a mindset: we see ourselves as the creative directors of our books, from inspiration to publication.

Our members may take a DIY self-publishing route, they may hire an assisted-publishing service, they may use a trade publisher for some of their projects but all understand that we are living in a golden age for writers and readers and they wish to enjoy the freedom, and accept the responsibility, of running their own show.

We use the terms "self"-publishing and "indie" author but these are relative terms, misnomers, really, in what is a highly collaborative business. To go indie is to become a team leader.

Nobody who produces a good book does so alone and publishing means partnership, often with a variety of individuals and organisations. The more people we reach with our work, the better. This guide is all about how to foster and develop good partnerships between self-publishing writers and those who work in the book trade and literary nonprofits.

#PublishingOpenUp

ALLi's *Open Up To Indie Authors* (#PublishingOpenUp) campaign includes a petition, lobbying of the industry, education seminars and now this guidebook by Debbie Young, ALLi's blog editor, and Dan Holloway, an ALLi community builder.

This book demonstrates through education and example how authors and various personnel in the industry — librarians, booksellers, reviewers, festival organisers and prize-giving committees — can successfully work together to the advantage of all. Its aims are threefold. To:

- equip self-published authors with the information and attitude they need to collaborate successfully with other players in the books and literary ecosystem.

- tackle the challenges of incorporating self-published books into literary organisations and events.

- raise awareness of the high quality and professional standards offered by the best self-publishing authors — and encourage their inclusion.

Our campaign urges the book and literary industries to incorporate more self-published books into their programmes. We know there are challenges in doing this and we have discussed them in detail throughout this book. Here I'd just like to address the challenge that traditional books people most often lament: the sheer size of the books market, now that "anyone" can publish, its exponential growth, and the consequent perceived difficulty of discovering good books among the bad.

The key to unlocking this challenge is very simple, as simple as a change of mindset. From scarcity thinking to abundance thinking; from commercial imperatives to creative.

Traditionally, publishing has worked from a scarcity model, grounded in commercial principles. It selected a very few books to be published and protected their value with copyright. Now we are working from an abundance model, grounded in creative principles.

In an abundance model, excess and redundancy are no cause for concern. This is how nature, the fundamental model for all creativity, works. An oak tree throws a lot of acorns to get one baby oak. A lot of sperm miss out on the egg.

But what about what one publishing executive recently referred to as "the mountains of crap"? It doesn't matter. Yes, self-publishing is enabling more poor-quality books to be published than ever before but in an abundance model what's important is not how many bad books are enabled — they quickly fall into invisibility as nobody reads them — but how many good books are enabled.

Throughout cultural history — in Italy during the Renaissance, in Elizabethan England, in transcendentalist America, in Literary Revival Ireland — whenever new creative forms and formats flourish, an opening up occurs. The means of expression becomes available to more people and, while this facilitates more tyro and aspirant work — our exec's "mountains of crap" — it also results in more accomplished and virtuoso work at the top. More masterpieces emerge, the expanded tip of that enlarged mountain.

The "problem" of book discoverability in the new publishing ecosystem is a fear created by an emotional or financial investment in the old order. It is not a problem for readers. Online algorithms are actually very effective — and getting better. From the reader's perspective, there's a book description, independent reader reviews, and a sample they can read before they buy. And book search through categories and keywords is far more effective as a discovery tool, if not as pleasant as the old method of bookstore browsing.

So good books are actually easier to find than they've ever been, including good self-published books, as Debbie and Dan so ably demonstrate in this guidebook.

The unprecedented wave of literary expression that self-publishing is facilitating is, actually, a beautiful thing when viewed through a creative, and not a critical or commercial, lens. Creativity is never orderly and neat; it's colourful and chaotic and kaleidoscopic and we need a publishing scene that acknowledges, and is prepared to be more reflective of, that truth.

To renege on that challenge because we don't like change — change in general, or the particular changes that are occurring in the industry — is to fail to serve the reading and writing community and to cut off great writing from the readership it deserves.

Sign Our Petition

ALLi's "Open Up To Indie Authors" campaign has a very simple aim: to remove discrimination against self-published books. If you support the aims of this campaign, please sign our petition on Change.org:

www.change.org/en-GB/petitions/open-up-to-indie-authors/

All of us at ALLi look forward to the day when this campaign, and this guide, will no longer be necessary.

Orna Ross
Director of The Alliance of Independent Authors (ALLi)
Open Up To Indie Authors Launch
The London Book Fair, 2014.

PART ONE

21st Century Publishing

I. Self-Publishing Today

Publishing has gone full circle. Historically writers, from medieval monks to Caxton to Swift, produced their own books. Then came the industrial revolution and market forces channelled most writers into the hands of dedicated commercial printing companies, many of which merged into large, powerful, global corporations such as Penguin-Random House.

Now, in the early 21st century, we can once more all be our own Caxton. Thanks to universally accessible, relatively affordable publishing technology, anyone can now publish a book – and set up a stall to sell it. Writers no longer need to win the hearts, minds and wallet of a traditional publishing company to reach readers.

No longer a corporate preserve, publishing is becoming increasingly democratised, now offering a dazzlingly array of opportunities, from the low-cost, ebook only approach, to the trade paperback, to sumptuous full-colour, coffee-table books whose retail price is in triple figures.

The development of print-on-demand technology has opened up much greater, affordable opportunities to print small runs, even single copies. Potentially, all the world's an author – and in control of their own authorial destiny. The internet and social media offer easy communication between publisher, author and reader, and digital publishing makes it possible to be a bestseller without printing a single physical copy if you want.

Used well, the sophisticated tools and services of the digital age enable authors to turn their own work into professional-looking, commercially viable books. The best are indistinguishable from those published by a big traditional publishing company. Detective work is often required to determine whether or not a book has been self-published. (Flicking through the last few pages to find the tell-tale credit for Lightning Source is one reliable but well-hidden sign.)

There are, of course, still authors who rush to push the "publish" button without making sure their book is the best it can be. Those who refuse to submit their golden words to proofreaders or even spellcheckers, either from artistic arrogance or from a lack of appreciation of the need. Those who have no idea that their book falls short of any standard of readability.

There will always be those who release onto an already seething marketplace books riddled with typos, bad content and poor cover designs that shriek "home-made", even at the thumbnail size displayed by online retailers. Not only advocates of traditional publishing cringe on sight of such books. Self-published authors producing books to a professional standard find it perhaps even more galling.

The Rise of the "Authorpreneur"

It is a rare author-publisher who physically performs every task required to produce a professional book, even if they have the necessary skills. Even a qualified proofreader, for example, would be unwise to check his own work, being too close to the text emotionally and creatively to spot typos.

The best self-publishers recognise their own strengths and weaknesses and surround themselves with a team of experts whose specialist skills complement the author's own. Indeed the term "self-publishing" is something of a misnomer, because there will almost certainly be others involved somewhere along the line.

The author's role in the publishing process is more one of creative director and business manager, rather than designer-cum-typesetter-cum-proofreader-cum-formatter-cum-marketeer.

The hybrid term "authorpreneur" is increasingly used to indicate an author of this type, one who does all of these things in a business-like and professional way, with the sophistication of a commercial publishing company but the freedom of the independent author.

Goodbye, Vanity Press; Hello, Author Services

Not all self-published authors wish to assume the mantle of the authorpreneur, especially if their prime objective is creative rather than commercial, but the high standards and reader reach they aim for will not be satisfied by old-fashioned vanity presses or jobbing printers, who, in return for a hefty fee, turn any manuscript into a print book without adding any value in terms of editing, proofreading or design.

There are plenty of options for authors who don't have the time, the will, or the skills to carry out all of the tasks required to publish their own book, from individual experts to assisted-publishing imprints run by experienced publishing professionals that offer the full range of facilities to supplement whatever skills the individual author lacks.

Cover and interior design, copy-editing, proofreading, ebook formatting: these and other services enable even the most time-pressed technophobe to produce a professional-looking book under the author's direction, at the author's expense.

While there are many excellent organisations and individuals who will help the self-published author produce a professional book at reasonable costs, there are also some over-priced and unscrupulous sharks who take advantage of the inexperienced author. Writer beware. (See Chapter Nine to find out about ALLi's Watchdog service which aims to expose and close down such operations.)

Alternatively the author may prefer to choose individual freelances specialising in whichever services they require, and there is a growing band of these available too. (ALLi's list of partner members is a good place to start shopping around. Again, see Chapter Nine for more about this list.)

Whichever option author-publishers choose, they need to read all contracts carefully, consider their goals in publication and retain as much control and return on investment as possible. Authors and those who wish to advise them well will find ALLi's companion guidebook in this series, *Choosing A Self-Publishing Service*, useful in enabling good choices.

The Rise of the Hybrid Author

When a self-publishing author reaches a certain level of success and visibility, they will find they agents and trade publishers come calling. Steena Holmes was picked up for an Amazon promotion that took her book from earning around $5,000 a month to over $100,000. Yes, per month.

Here Steena talks about her decision to add a trade publishing deal to her author-publishing life and that, contrary to the expectations of many, that did not mean she was no longer an indie author:

I love being a self-published author and was in the middle of putting together a launch for my new book to follow my first bestseller, Finding Emma *when I started to receive offers and [at first] I was caught off guard. Thanks to ALLi, however, I knew what my goals were as an author and I knew what questions I wanted answered by both agent and publisher before I took any steps forward. My number one question was whether they would support my self-publishing goals.*

Being an indie is no longer about choosing between being self-published or trade-published. Indie authors can embrace both. Could I continue to see the success I have on my own? Absolutely. There are so many successful indie authors who choose that way.

But whichever way we do it, if we want to be career authors, we need to start considering our career path as a business. That's another thing I learned from ALLi.

As indies, we already work with cover artists, editors and marketing experts and use their knowledge to help us launch our books and find new readers. So the idea of working with an agent or publisher should be no different... As an indie author, I can have the best of both worlds.
Steena Holmes

ALLi agrees with this broad definition of "independent author". The defining quality of the organisation is its inclusiveness and diversity of approach and all who want to self-publish a book well are welcomed. It defines as "indie" all authors who see themselves as the creative directors of their own books, from concept to completion; who are independent in attitude and responsible for their own publishing choices and destiny, no matter which type of publishing service they use — paid or trade.

Other indie authors are reluctant to accept a trade publishing offer, being unwilling to relinquish the artistic and marketing freedom of self-publishing. When Steena published her thoughts above on ALLi's Self-Publishing Advice Blog, I (Dan) replied with my own credo:

The key point for me lies in Steena's tack-change half way through her compelling piece, predicated on that conditional, "if you want a writing career". My decision to self-publish was based largely on the fact I didn't want a writing career. I would positively hate having a writing career.

I would have to write the kind of thing that just doesn't come naturally to me...I've written a thriller. One that's sold thousands of copies and has been a staff pick of the year at one of the UK's most famous bookshops. But writing it was like having my teeth pulled. And trying to write the sequel was like trying to conjure new teeth from the raw, bleeding pits where those teeth once were -- and pulling them again.

I can't do it. I don't enjoy it. And I'm not particularly good at it.

In other words, to make a career at writing I would have to turn it into a day job. And I won't do that. Next to my wife, my cats, and my rats, writing is my great joy in life, and I want to keep it that way.

Not that I'm not ambitious. I'm hugely ambitious. I want to leave my mark on the cultural landscape for generations to come. I want to change lives, to change societies even, with my words.

I want to change the way people think about words themselves. I won't, of course. I'm not good enough. But it is my ambition. And the key thing is: whilst I'm not good enough to make a career writing thrillers, trying to do it gives me no pleasure. But whilst I'm not good enough to change literature, the attempt is a delight.

Self-publishing gives me the freedom to do what I love and to push at any boundary I want with no considerations other than the writing.

Dan Holloway

Another ALLi member, Indian author-publisher Rasana Atreya is open in principle but has turned down offers to date and is confident this has been the right decision for her.

Around the time the unpublished manuscript of my novel, Tell A Thousand Lies, *was shortlisted for the 2012 Tibor Jones South Asia Award, I was also offered a publishing contract by a mainstream publisher here in India. I checked out their top performing books – sales for their print books in India were amazing, but they had barely any presence on Amazon, ebook-wise. I asked them if they'd let me keep my ebook rights. They refused. Considering that they were offering me 5% in royalties (with an average advance), and weren't doing anything with ebooks, I decided I could do better for myself.*

For a first-time author this wasn›t an easy decision; my friends thought I was nuts, but it turns out this was the best thing I ever did. Most months I make more money than the advance they offered. In that publisher›s defence, the advance was in Indian rupees, and was not bad. But 95% of my sales are in the US/UK market, so the exchange rate works in my favour.

Rasana Atreya, Indian novelist

Movement in the other direction is equally common, with authors starting out as trade-published but side-stepping into self-publishing, for a variety of different reasons. Perhaps they are dissatisfied with the way a publisher handled their work; they're squeezed out through lack of sales or, increasingly, because they realise that self-publishing offers greater freedom and power to follow their own creative ambitions. ALLi's founder, the Irish novelist and poet Orna Ross, falls into this category:

The single best thing I ever did in my writing life was decide to self-publish a book as an experiment. I'd worked in publishing and media for twenty years and I loved lots about that work, so I wasn't sure if author-publishing would be right for me. I started small, with a poetry book and then a meditation manual, on the basis that they wouldn't be too widely read if I made a mess of it all. I didn't really expect anyone to buy them.

But they did, not in huge numbers but after all, it was poetry and meditation. So I took the plunge and got the rights to my novels back from my publisher.

I was one of those many writers who hadn't liked the treatment given to my books (where I saw family dramas that brought readers through emotional and thought-provoking twists and turns, my publisher saw chick-lit). So I have been reissuing the books, in different formats, with the titles and treatment I had originally envisaged *when writing them.*

Pressing that "Save & Publish" button on the first of these revamped books was one of the most joyous moments of my life. Heady!

Orna Ross, Irish novelist and poet

Alternatively, it may be a simple commercial decision. Hugh Howey, having achieved tremendous sales of his ebooks, when offered a trade publishing contract, would only consent for print books, retaining his ebook rights and continuing the practice which had already served him well. If it ain't broke…

More and more writers are keeping a foot in both camps. They may continue to have some books trade-published while branching off in new directions with self-published titles that their current publisher doesn't wish to commission, perhaps because they are in a different genre than usual, or because they are outside of the publisher's usual portfolio. British medical broadcaster, journalist and academic Dr Carol Cooper has many medical and healthcare books to her credit, but she chose to self-publish her first novel, for example.

Increasingly, trade-published authors are using self-publishing facilities to revive backlist titles that their trade publishing house has allowed to go out of print. When *USA Today* bestselling novelist Helen Hollick's British publishers decided to drop her backlist, on the dubious grounds that historical novels were falling out of fashion, Helen decided to self-publish in the UK, while remaining trade-published on the other side of the Atlantic.

As any indie authors who have fallen foul of a trade publishing house's change of heart will tell you, self-published books – unlike their trade counterpart – have no sell-by date. The author may market for as long as he or she wishes, whereas the trade publisher will likely tire of supporting a book that isn't selling in large numbers. In the world of ebooks and print-on-demand, all books are immortal. They need never go out of print or get pulped to make room in the publisher's warehouse for the next big thing. Self-published authors have no "time's winged chariot" at their back... other than their own mortality.

On re-acquiring their books' rights and self-publishing their backlist, many previously trade-published authors are often pleasantly surprised to discover that with self-publishing comes a much higher profit margin. The typical author's cut of 35%–70% of retail price for an ebook is a substantial improvement from the typical 5 -15% of a trade-published print book.

There are many other significant freedoms. They now have the opportunity to change titles, cover designs, or even some of the content of the books, no longer constrained by their publisher's — or, more likely these days — the chain store or supermarket buyers' preferences.

Every Author's Goal: Reaching Readers

It's clear that self-publishing and trade-published books can coexist comfortably side by side in an author's portfolio. No matter how their books are published, every author seeks readers, and there are many ways of reaching them:

- Retailers

- Reviewers

- Libraries

- Festivals

- Awards

- Professional associations

- Word of mouth recommendation

It seems reasonable that books of equal quality should be treated on equal terms in all of these spheres, no matter how they have been published. It is therefore a source of frustration and disappointment to self-published authors who have produced a top-quality book to encounter glass-ceilings or dead-ends along simply because they have managed its production themselves.

The fault is not all on the side of the establishment. Among certain self-published authors, there exists an assumption that simply publishing a book gives them *de facto* equal rights in the marketplace with trade-published bestsellers, an assumption that is not realistic for those who have produced a poor quality book.

It's one thing to have your book rejected because it is not good enough: shoddy cover, dreadful content, or copy full of typos. To have it rejected because of the lack of a trade publisher's name on the spine, even though it's a match for trade-published books in every other respect, feels uncomfortably like snobbery or literary prejudice.

But self-published authors may do much to help their own cause. First, they should be open-minded about their prospects and not assume prejudice before they meet it: it may not happen. They also need to be realistic. They are unlikely to have the length and breadth of experience enjoyed by a trade publishing company, so they need to gain a clear understanding of how the book trade and all the associated operations work. With realistic expectations, they will meet less disappointment – for example, if they are familiar with the retailers' standard expectations for trade discount but are unwilling to meet them, they should not feel hard done by if their local bookshop refuses to stock their books.

Equally, the publishing trade needs to recognise and respect the high quantity of high quality books now being self-published. The next chapter will therefore offer easy ways to identify self-published books of all kinds, to help other members of the book trade make informed, rather than pre-conceived, judgements.

2. How to Find Great Self-published Books

FIRST, FIND YOUR Self-Published Book! Echoing the apocryphal beginning of Georgian chef Hannah Glasse's recipe for jugged hare, "First, catch your hare", it is not as easy as it ought to be to find self-published books.

Largely excluded from books-and-mortar stores and from festivals, events, public libraries and most literary awards, self-published books are not exactly high profile offline. That's not because, as is sometimes assumed, they only exist in digital form. There are plenty of self-published print books in existence – it's just that the best ones are indistinguishable from trade-published books and do do not identify themselves.

In the bookshops that stock self-published books, they nestle on the shelves among trade-published peers, camouflaged by their quality. Bookstores usually display self-published books in among their main stock, not in a separate section, unless particularly highlighting them as books by local authors and publishers.

Indie bookshops are more likely to stock them than bookstore chains, given their shared independent spirit, unconstrained by head office policy.

While there exist online stores that stock exclusively self-published books, such as http://www.libiro.com, in bricks-and-mortar stores, there's less likely to be obvious discrimination, whether positive or negative. After all, few of their customers will be specifically looking for self-published work – they're just after good books.

Checking Credentials

When you come across a new book from an unfamiliar source – perhaps one that you've been sent as a free sample for consideration – it may not be obvious whether or not it is self-published. Yes, there are some clear pointers, such as if the author has simply put his own name down as publisher on the spine or in the copyright section, or has used a company name obviously allied to his personal name. However, many self-published authors choose to set up their own micro-publishing company or at least use a "trading-as" name, even if they publish only their own books, because a different name and a corporate logo on the jacket adds a professional touch. Finnish novelist Helena Halme, for example, uses the imprint Newhurst Press, which publishes exclusively her own, very beautiful, books.

Some self-published authors go a step further and band together to form a collective. Triskele Books is an international cooperative of six authors – Jasper Dorgan (in England), Gillian E. Hamer (in Wales), J.J. Marsh (in Switzerland), Liza Perrat (in France), J. D. Smith (in England) and Catriona Troth (in England). Working together gives them many other advantages besides a shared branding.

Another significant proportion of self-published authors employ author service providers to carry out the design and production process for their books, with the service provider playing the role of publisher, funded by the author. SilverWood Books, for example, provides such services to authors around the world, whose books are then officially published under the SilverWood Books imprint.

Checking the publisher's credentials, then, is not a clear-cut way of identifying which books are self-published, but it is a helpful starting point.

Online Research

The next step is to research the book online. If it's retailing anywhere other than the author's own website, it will be on Amazon. You don't have to be an Amazon customer or supporter to take advantage of their vast public database of books, the largest and most comprehensive in the world. Many bricks-and-mortar stores who find Amazon anathema still use its website as a useful information resource.

Go to the Amazon website that serves your territory and search the author, title or ISBN of the book. (If you're not sure which Amazon website to use, head for www.amazon.com, which will recognise your origin and suggest the appropriate URL for your location.

Few self-published books are not listed on Amazon. Only a small number of self-published authors will avoid them, perhaps for reasons of politics or principle, or because they wish only to hand-sell their books, or to distribute them via their own website to their own circle of trusted readers.

The book's listing on Amazon will give you plenty of evidence to help you judge the book's quality in the following areas:

- Cover image.

- Book description, the equivalent to the blurb on the jacket, plus often a lot more useful info, including pre-publication reviews – the space allowed is quite generous.

- Current bestseller sales rank (NB: indicative only for sales made via Amazon and in the territory covered by the particular Amazon site you are viewing and only logged once the book has sold a small number of copies).

- Reviews submitted to the Amazon site viewed, plus a count of and link to reviews left on the largest site, Amazon.com.

- A link to the author profile held by Amazon's AuthorCentral service, provided that the author has completed this in file for the territory you're viewing.

- Name of publisher.

- Date of publication.

- Number of pages.

- Size of print book, if available.

- The opportunity to "look inside" and read the first few pages or a random selection of pages of the text.

- For ebooks, the chance to download a free sample to your Kindle or Kindle app on a non-Amazon device (PC, laptop, tablet, phone, etc.) to read at your leisure.

- Availability from Amazon and approved Amazon partners (including second-hand copies).

Judging Self-Published Books By Their Covers

Looking first at the cover, it will be difficult to distinguish the very best self-published books from their trade-published peers, because their authors will have engaged experts and specialists to provide a professional-looking, genre-appropriate, visually appealing and effective cover, visible at thumbnail size online. These experts are likely also to be working for the big trade publishing companies, offering the same quality to both kinds of customer. This makes it hard for the shopper to spot which is which.

For reasons of low budget or poor judgement, some self-published authors decline to consider design. It's easy to pick out such covers, with their illegible fonts, ill-chosen titles, garish colours and poor quality photos or amateurish illustrations. Or indeed, there may be nothing on the cover at all to indicate its genre, simply the name and title on a blank background in an inappropriate font.

Seasoned Amazon shoppers will quickly learn to spot self-published books with covers made from templates offered by Amazon's KDP self-publishing package. These templates allow authors to put together their own cover design at no cost. In the right hands, someone with a natural eye for good design and the vernacular of their genre, these templates can be effective. In the wrong hands, they leap off the screen shouting "amateur!"

Looking Inside

Amazon, Kobo and other e-tailers make it easy to sample the text of the book, so that potential purchasers can try before they buy. This can be done in two ways: the first is by clicking the "Look Inside" button, which enables you to read the first few pages of text. Alternatively, Amazon offers its customers the facility to download completely free of charge – and with no obligation to buy – a substantial free sample of the book.

You can actually do this on a number of books without ever having to make a purchase, setting up an account solely for this purpose, even if you don't own an Amazon-compatible e-reader (Kindle). You can instead read your free samples on other electronic devices for which free Kindle apps are available – smartphones, tablets, laptops, and PCs.

At the end of each sample is an invitation to download the rest of the book immediately, with the cost to be charged to your account. Don't worry if you hit the "accept" button by mistake, Amazon will cancel your purchase and make a refund within a short timeframe to allow for slips of the finger.

The free sample is usually sufficient to allow the reader to get a feel for the content: whether it's well written, well formatted, free of error, with content that's enticing to you. So sorting the wheat from the chaff is easy.

Third Party Evidence: Readers' Reviews

For further input, it's worth reading the reviews that readers have left on Amazon, although these should never be taken entirely at face value. Amazon has taken pains to minimise abuse of the review system, but some does still get through, e.g. writers or publishers setting up bogus accounts to review their own books.

Even a cursory glance at the reviews will almost always be helpful in determining the value of a book. The star rating is not always helpful, as different readers allocate their ratings differently. A rave review filled with unstinting praise may carry only three stars, for example, if that particular reviewer only gives 4* or 5* in exceptional circumstances, while some 5* reviews sound less enthusiastic, written by reviewers who give 5* to everything they buy, unless it's really disappointing.

Equally, check that a low rating has been given for the right reasons: a delivery failure, or the reader having mistakenly ordered the wrong book, often results in a disgruntled 1* review. It's always worth reading the other reviews left by any reader whose report sounds unnatural or unlikely. Your findings may make you decide to disregard what that person has said, if all their reviews are very scathing or unstinting in their praise, or if they've only reviewed books by one author.

There is also a growing number of reader reviews on other online retailers such as Kobo, whose elegant book review sections are very easy on the eye; on the websites of bricks-and-mortar chains; and on social media designed for readers' discussion of books, most notably Goodreads.

Although Goodreads is now owned by Amazon, the two sites feature different reviews. There is a lot of overlap between Goodreads networkers and Amazon books customers and some, but most certainly not all, post the same review on both sites. It will be interesting to see how both sites develop as their merger settles down.

Wherever you choose to examine readers' reviews, bear in mind that these are just individual customer viewpoints rather than professional criticism, although there are plenty of gifted, insightful reviewers on all of such sites.

Book Evaluation Sites

Another, and perhaps more detached view, may come from "book evaluation" sites, which engage qualified reviewers to sit in judgement on books submitted by self-published authors.

One such is Awesome Indies, founded by Tahlia Newland because, she says, "I was so frustrated with buying books with good star-ratings only to discover that they were so badly written I couldn't finish them."

On such sites, authors are invited to submit their books and those deemed worthy are awarded a badge as an indicator of professional quality. For books that don't make the grade, the organisations offer guidance on improvements required to meet their stringent standard. Thus they are not only indicating when high standards are found in self-published books, they are also helping to raise the bar.

Submission to some of these programmes is free, others charge so they are able to compensate their reviewers for their time and effort but medallions may not be bought: they can only be earned by the production of a self-published book that meets professional standards.

Some of the sites also gain recompense for their services via affiliate links to online retailers for the books that they have reviewed.

While it may be worth looking out for such a badge, the absence of such a seal of approval does not indicate that a self-published book is not of high quality. Firstly, the use of book evaluation sites is optional, and only a small proportion of self-publishing authors go through that process. Secondly, they are rating books against the standards and expectations for trade-published books. They are not geared up for appreciating less commercial work, such as experimental writing or highly literary fiction, for which self-publishing is such an important outlet.

Other Awards

Many industry book award schemes are not open to self-published books at all. The Australian novelist Elisabeth Storrs, whose trade-published debut novel was nominated for awards found her second book automatically disqualified from her country's Prime Minister's Literary Award because it was self-published, for no apparent reason other than prejudice.

ALLi members have been rejected from many such schemes with blunt and unsubstantiated statements from organisers who claim "we'd just be inundated with rubbish". Some awards are exclusively open to the self-published books and uphold high standards. Any holders of the respected Rubery Award, for example, should be considered to have a quality endorsement. New for 2014 is the Quagga Prize, reserved for self-published novels, with a special award for literary fiction.

Sadly, other schemes have been devised to prey on the hopes and aspirations of naïve self-published authors, requiring substantial entry fees for little return. To check the value of an award, it's best to visit the organiser's website, read the terms and conditions, and look at past winners. If the gallery of winners is filled with ugly, unprofessional looking covers, or there are as many winners as entrants, the award is most likely a scam. As always, you can check with ALLi's Watchdog Desk if in doubt.

Author Websites

Further evidence of the author's skills and professionalism may be found on his or her website. Any self-published authors who take their writing and their need to market their book seriously will have set up some kind of online presence. The copy on their blog or home page will be a reliable indicator of the quality of their writing elsewhere.

Free Review Copies

Of course, all of these activities are no substitute for actually buying and reading the whole of a book to assess it in its entirely. If you're seriously considering stocking or promoting a self-published book in any way, and want to try before you buy, ask the author if they'd be prepared to offer you a free preview copy. The author's willingness to part with a copy for serious evaluation will indicate his or her faith in the quality of their own book and the earnestness of their intention to do business with you.

Writers' Organisations

Another useful indicator of any author's professional intent is whether he or she belongs to a serious organisation for writers. As will be discussed later in this book, many long-established authors' societies do not yet permit self-published authors to join, considering them not "officially published" without the endorsement of a trade publishing contract, even if as a self-published author they have sold thousands of books and gained hundreds of enthusiastic reviews from readers.

Or they may permit them to join, but only in a separate category, as an Associate member or other "not-yet-published" category.

The Alliance of Independent Authors (ALLi) takes a different approach: any published writer may join at the Author Member level, whether self-published, trade-published, or a mixture of both. ALLi also has a professional membership for author-publishers who are making a living from their work. While membership of the Alliance is not in itself proof of the quality of the author's books, it does indicate a writer's serious intent to self-published to professional standards.

ALLi also seeks to give voice and greater visibility to the self-published author within an increasingly crowded book trade. The organisation showcases a sample of top quality self-published books in all genres in its new awards scheme, highlighted on its home page. These books are nominated by readers for their excellence and foregrounded by ALLi's team of reviewers.

Chapter Nine provides an overview of how the organisation is working to help self-published authors work more closely with the established book trade, to raise standards, share best practices and create an ever-higher quality standard of self-publishing, to everyone's benefit.

ISBNS

Finally, a note to authors. If you want you book to be stocked by libraries and bookstores, it's advisable for you to purchase your own ISBNs from whichever body allocates them in your country.

An ISBN is an individual number allocated to your book in a particular format. It's how a librarian or somebody on the till in a bookstores ensures they are buying the pbook, for example, not the ebook.

The entire book trade uses ISBNs as identifiers so if you want to be included in trade systems, you need to allocate a unique ISBN to each format of each title that you publish.

ALLi recommends that you purchase your own ISBNs, rather than relying on the free ones allocated by service providers like Createspace or Smashwords. At a minimum, allocate one ISBN to your ebook, one to pbook, and one to audiobook for each title. You may, as some of our members do, want to give a different ISBN to your .mobi (Amazon) file and your .epub, or to your POD edition of your book and a print run for bookshop distribution.

Both Bowker (US) and Neilsen (UK), two of the major ISBN allocators, sell them in batches of ten or one hundred, though in other countries, they may be free. Owning your own ISBNs means you are the publisher of record for those titles and allows the books to be tracked back to you.

3. About The #PublishingOpenUp Campaign

IN 2012, A new global organisation for self-publishers was founded by Orna Ross, novelist, poet and lecturer in creative and imaginative process.

Ross was previously published nonfiction with Attic Press, an independent Dublin-based publisher for her nonfiction, and fiction with Penguin but had begun to publish her own work, because she sought greater creative freedom than that offered by her publisher. Re-acquiring the rights to her backlist, she now self-publishes novels, poetry and books about creativity, to commercial success and critical acclaim.

Working independently made her realise that self-published authors operating in isolation would benefit from a non-profit organization to unite them in a spirit of mutual support and as-sistance. An online organisation would enable "indie authors", as they were coming to be called, and their advisors to communicate easily across continents, to share best practice and advice, and help each other in developing the self-publishing sector along more professional, organised lines, integrating those writers who wanted a presence into the existing book infrastructure — bookstores, libraries, literary festivals, prizes.

"As well as giving the individual author support to self-publish well and reach their reader, our vision was that our members would work together to raise awareness and respect for the self-publishing option," says Ross today. "One of our aims is to build mutually supportive relationships between self-published authors and all those who influence their success: the media, retailers, reviewers, festival organisers, award schemes and other professional bodies. It can be daunting for an individual writer, especially if they meet with condescension or hostility but together, we gain strength in numbers."

ALLi welcomes all those who are on the self-publishing journey, whether still aspiring and not yet self-published (as Associate Members); already self-published in any form (as Author Members); or self-publishing so successfully that it earns them their living (as Professional Members). There's also a category for the associated companies and services that help them create their books (as Partners).

The organisation's attitude to applicants and members is as inclusive as it is possible to be, also welcoming trade-published authors who seek to self-publish, "hybrid" authors whose aim is to flourish in both spheres, and self-published authors whose success earns them trade publishing contracts, for those who wish to move in that direction. And, of course, to be an support and advocate for the increasing number of authors who are coming to prefer the self-publishing option, reluctant as they are to relinquish the independence and the greater income it allows.

During the first year of ALLi's operation, Orna Ross enlisted the support of established experts in the field of self-publishing to form a valuable central resource. This includes specialists in literary values, creativity, book design, marketing, distribution, rights and other legal issues, finance and business management. She also assembled a core support team to nurture its members and disseminate ALLi's messages effectively through all available routes, including a website, an advice blog and social media.

Since its launch, ALLi's membership has grown substantially, adding members from English-speaking territories all around the globe: Africa, the Americas, Australasia, Europe and the UK.

Campaigning activity is now stepping up to the next level. Having demonstrated that self-publishing is a viable option for authors to produce high quality books, it is now devoting much energy to its"Open Up To Indie Authors" campaign, to encourage equal opportunities for all writers of equal merit.

Petition

To demonstrate the collective will for such attitudes to change, ALLi has formulated a petition, addressed to various personnel in the book and publishing ecosystem, with its addressees regularly changed. It reads:

I, and the Alliance of Independent Authors, urge you to find ways to include self-publishing writers as a matter of priority.

As you know, more and more writers are turning to self-publishing and many such authors are producing work of proven value to readers.

While recognising that there are challenges in incorporating indie authors, it has become a necessity, if book stores, libraries, literary events and reviewers are to be inclusive of writers. And fully serving readers.

I trust you will give this matter the attention it deserves.

With thanks,

Sincerely,

[Your name]

The link is: http://www.change.org/en-GB/petitions/open-up-to-indie-authors/. If you have not yet signed the petition, please do – and spread the word.

Responses To The Campaign

Already the campaign is having some effects, with various book-sellers, librarians, prize giving committees, events organisers and reviewers setting up structures that allow them work with self-pub-lishing writers. And in some quarters, most noticeably the new publishing platforms, the campaign is pushing an open door.

Here is Mark Lefebvre, Director of Self-Publishing & Author Relations at Kobo, and himself an author (as Mark Leslie) and former bookseller.

I think the "Open Up To Indie Authors" program is an important one. Having worked as a bookseller for twenty years, I recognise the critical role that local booksellers and librarians play in the role of supporting local authors.

What booksellers take great pleasure in is when they are able to put the right books into the right customer's hands at the right time. When that happens, magic happens.

It is not a simple business transaction, but part of a wonderful relationship of sharing and trust.

One of the most satisfying experiences I have had as a bookseller involve discovering a brilliant local writer and sharing their work with customers I know would really enjoy them. It doesn't matter who published the book or where it is from. What matters is not just that the book is a good one, but an excellent choice for THAT customer.

Any program that helps introduce booksellers and authors is one that will further enrich reading culture globally.

When I speak with authors, I regularly remind them of the importance of embracing their local bookstore, getting to know the people who work there.

The Kobo Writing Life team has already begun campaigns designed to bring indie authors and local booksellers together, demonstrating that, working together, they can really help one another out. We have hosted, in collaboration with local booksellers, events in London, Toronto, New York and Portland so far, and are looking forward to doing much more.

Kobo is eager to work with ALLi on the "Open Up to Indie Authors" program and publication, thereby continuing to assist authors with navigating the critical yet often complex layers, relationships and processes surrounding the book industry.

Mark Lefebvre,
Director of Self-Publishing & Author Relations at Kobo Books.

Through Kobo's links with retail partners like WH Smith in the UK or the American Bookseller's Association in the US, ALLi members are enabled to launch their books, in conjunction with this guidebook, in their local bookstore. And all self-publishing writers are given access to Kobo's distribution partners on four continents, with over 10,000 retail outlets and access to over 100 million consumers. This access will continue to grow as Kobo expands its network.

Like just about every aspect of publishing in the 21st century, attitudes to self-published authors are evolving fast. This campaign and handbook aim to hasten and shape that evolution to the advantage of all.

Section II of this book, Fostering Equal Opportunities, now offers the self-published author advice on how to gain the best chance of inclusion in the literary and publishing ecosystem on an equal footing. We will address in turn the most important bodies that help determine the success and acceptance of authors everywhere:

- Retailers.

- Reviewers.

- Libraries

- Festivals and events.

- Awards and prizes.

- Associations and Societies.

PART TWO

Equal Opportunities For All Books

4. Book Retailers

Bricks-and-mortar bookstores

For many authors, there's nothing like seeing your book on display in a bricks-and-mortar bookstore. To even the most ardent ebook fan, getting a print book stocked by a physical bookstore is the mark of a credible author. Rightly or wrongly, securing an in-store signing event can make an author feel that he or she has really "arrived".

Ask any author, whether trade- or self-published, to describe their ideal relationship with their local high street or shopping mall retailer, and they are likely to describe this scenario:

- A book that is seen from the street, with a shop window display to catch the eye of passers-by, luring them in with the sight of your book.

- Inside the store, a large stack of your books, stacked cover uppermost on a display table in the store's main route for traffic, near the entrance.

- A supply of your promotional bookmarks or postcards on the counter to catch the eye of anyone who has managed to make it to the till without spotting your book.

- Sales advisors who are familiar with your book, having read it themselves, who will gladly act as salesmen on your behalf.

After all, what a great job bookstore staff must have, being surrounded all day by books they love, hooking them up with eager readers who will love them too and be grateful for their support, right?

The Reality of Retailing

Those window displays and table-top displays every author covets? In chains, these are usually bought and paid for, at a substantial price, by big trade publishing companies for books that are likely to repay their investment many times over. Often these will be books by mammoth-selling authors, possibly celebrities, or high profile authors for other reasons. For example, spin-offs from a top TV show or movie, as highlighted in the Guardian article Publish and Be Branded: The New Threat to Literature's Laboratory.

In independent bookshops, where the proprietor's displays are not dictated or funded by head office deals, there will be more freedom and flexibility, but the bookseller will still need a very compelling reason to give your book that top spot – namely, the prospect of runaway sales and profit.

Just because you are a local resident and a regular customer does not earn your book the right to take up shop space. What does, is its potential and actual sales – and it's down to you to convince the stores that your book has wings.

The restricted counter space by the till is usually reserved for high-margin, last-minute impulse buys (bookmarks, gadgets, stationery, book tokens) to boost the average customer's spend in store and so enhance the shop's profit. Shop counters are not free advertising space. If you're itching to give away your stash of bookmarks, they'll be better used elsewhere, such as public libraries, festivals and other events.

Store staff are busy, stressed and pressed for time. They'll be receiving frequent deliveries of stock to be put away, and regular visits from trade publishers' salesmen giving them a speedy pitch for dozens of books at a time, at around ten seconds per book. Sure, they'll have some appreciative, regular customers who brighten up their day, but they'll also have a lot of tricky, dissatisfied customers to contend with.

Though likely to be avid readers in their own time, they may not be personally interested in your genre or sufficiently sold on it themselves to buy to read at home. They certainly don't get to read books all day, any more than a bakery assistant spends his day eating free cakes. (Though if you're on friendly terms with any member of your local bookstore's staff, offering them a free complimentary copy of your book may not be a bad idea, if their company policy allows them to accept it.)

To share a little of their experience, read Jen Campbell's *Weird Things Customers Say In Bookshops* and its sequel. This will help you imagine what it would be like to be on the receiving end all day every day of questions such as "Is there a sequel to The Diary of Anne Frank?" or wanting to return a copy of Where's Wally? "because I've found him".

The typical sales advisor's day does not allow copious amounts of time to deal with individual authors who pitch up unannounced to chat at length about their latest book. On average, high street booksellers are approached at least once every day by a self-published author. That's a lot of time each week in an already demanding job in an area of the economy having to work incredibly hard to stay afloat.

What's more, some bookstores feel that they have been 'burned' by self-publishers in the past and don't want to risk it again. One bookshop owner of our acquaintance took on a pile of an author's books after striking up a conversation with him and displayed them prominently. Days after he started selling them enthusiastically, customers began coming in to complain about substandard production. Now he is wary of ever touching a self-published book again.

Chain Stores versus Independents

It's reasonable to assume that independent bookstores will be more sympathetic to the lot of the self-published author because they both value independence. In that they are not answerable to any head office directives, independent bookstores do have more freedom, but that doesn't allow them to stock just any book without first being sure it makes economic sense, or to be blindly supportive of any other entity that flourishes the word "independent" or "local" as if it's a secret handshake or a magic key to the door.

Just like the big chains, independent bookstores must make money. They may not have to accommodate pressure from shareholders or the stock-market, but to remain in business, they must at least break even. The sad demise of far too many independent bookstores in recent years demonstrates the difficulty of their task.

Independent of spirit they may be, but selling books at a profit is still their livelihood. When I (Debbie) was researching my book promotion handbook for self-published authors, *Sell Your Books!*, I interviewed the proprietor of two independent bookshops near where I live. The two-store Yellow-Lighted Bookshop chain is owned by the enterprising, free-spirited Hereward Corbett, who, before turning independent, held senior positions in major British bookstore chains. He told me: "I love my job and I love books, but at the end of the day, I have my mortgage to pay." Can't argue with that!

No matter how much bookstore proprietors value their independence, unless they are eccentric millionaires who are to writers as Marie Antoinette was to shepherdesses, they are driven by an unforgiving financial imperative. Unlike many self-published authors, they don't have a day job to fund their involvement with self-publishing, however sympathetic they may feel.

Self-Published versus Trade-Published

Undoubtedly, booksellers still feel more comfortable buying their stocks from trade publishers' salesmen who tout 100+ books on every visit than from a self-published author turning up with just the one. Trade publishers provide the assurance of quality control: their stock is a safe investment. Trade publishers also make the necessary administration easy for the bookseller, with a single invoice for hundreds of books and authors, payable directly, with a handsome discount (usually around 40%) and the agreement to provide these top quality books on a sale or return basis, no questions asked.

If your self-published book has been rejected by a bookstore, it's very easy to play the offended card and blame those old demons, "The Gatekeepers", but hold fire. Many trade-published authors also despair of getting their books stocked in-store, elbowed out, as they see it, by the big names on which trade publishers focus most of their marketing spend.

The average trade-published author does not necessarily have an advantage over the average self-published. The self-published author, acting alone, will always be more demanding of the bookseller's time in proportion to the number of books sold, no matter how efficiently you work. On the other hand, the self-published author will also always have certain advantages over the trade-published author.

The Self-Published Author's Advantages

- The commercial freedom to represent themselves, on their own terms, rather than being governed by a commercial publishing contract.

- The acceptance of the need to carry out the hands-on marketing of their own book themselves.

- The drive and passion to do all in their power to market it – without this passion, they'd never have made it to the finishing line of self-publishing their own book in the first place.

- The sense of responsibility for their book's marketing.

- A growing sophistication and ability to market their book – the best indies are much more commercially aware and savvy than the average trade-published author.

- The power to negotiate directly and make their own decisions.

All of these advantages ought to be welcomed by the bookstore buyer or proprietor. So self-published authors should introduce themselves to local booksellers and ask if they are willing to sell books on consignment. In this arrangement, the store carries a few copies of the book and if it sells, the author and store split the earnings -- at 50/50 or some other pre-determined rate.

Unlike in a traditional distribution arrangement where the bookstore pays for the books upfront and is refunded for those that don't sell, books sold on consignment only cost the owner shelf space.

It's up to the individual author to make those benefits clear to them.

How To Give Your Book The Best Chance of Being Stocked By A Bookstore

There are basics you must take care of to ensure a bookstore or library buyer will treat you with as much consideration as a trade-published author.

> ~ **Match Professional Quality.** First and foremost, before you go anywhere near a bookstore, make sure your book is the very best it can possibly be. Of course, this should have happened before you hit the "publish" button, but if you haven't, and your book will stand out as "self-published" in the setting of a bookstore, you are backing a loser. If you put your book in an identity parade alongside trade-published books, would anyone be able to pick it out as the villain? It's down to you to make sure that they cannot.

> Bear in mind that many indie booksellers are keen, in principle, to support self-published authors, but they can only do so with a decent product that stands a good chance of commercial success, as indicated by Scottish-Canadian novelist Catriona Troth's conversation with the proprietors of one award-winning independent bookstore: "When I asked them about stocking self-published books, they exchanged a look. 'We do take books from self-published authors, on sale or return', I was told. 'And some are very good. But some are awful, just dreadful. You could never promote them. The look of some of the books … We try to be encouraging, but it's hard.'"

> Catriona's books met their required standards and are now selling well from that shop's shelves, and she's also purposefully driving traffic to the shop with her own PR. Make sure you do the same with yours.

> ~ **A Good Jacket.** Your book's genre should be evident at a glance from the look of its cover, and it should sit comfortably alongside other books similar in nature.

> No matter how superlative its content, your book will never, ever appear on a display table or even front-facing on a shelf

if it looks like the hangover following a night of Photoshop and Clipart cocktails. That's the one thing they can't hide, the thing that affects how their pride and joy – their bookstore – looks. Remember how angry you were at people suggesting ridiculous things for your cover? That's how a bookshop owner feels at the thought of having an awful cover on display.

~ **Size matters.** Trade paperbacks are usually 8" x 5.5", but many self-published books are less usual sizes, such as 9" x 6" because of the different print sources used for production. This may not matter to some retailers, but others will reject outright oddities that will make their shelves look untidy. Think before you print.

~ **Appropriate Interior Design.** Interior layout, though obviously not visible from afar, is also important. Unprofessional or unsuitable typography is an instant giveaway of an amateur book. Be sure to consider the following when having your book typeset:

- typeface – is it legible, clear, and consistent, with an appropriate font choice for the subject and target reader? Many of the fonts that are popular for word processing, like Times New Roman or Arial, do not work well for print.

- pagination – are the page numbers discreet, the right size, and where they should be?

- margins – are they justified, as in trade published books?

- gutters – are they wide enough to make the book easy to read?

- professional finish – is it free of typos, rogue spaces, and odd line breaks?

- See http://www.bookdesigntemplates.com/ for more on this and a free book construction manual from ALLi Design Advisor, Joel Friedlander.

On her first brush with self-publishing, *USA Today* bestseller Helen Hollick was aghast to discover that the first author services provider she used typeset her book in the font in which she'd written her draft: Comic Sans. Needless to say, she swiftly moved on to a more professional partner!

If you can say yes, hand on heart, to all of these questions, you can present your book with professional pride. If not, you are not giving your book its best chance. All of these things are within your control, but only if you are prepared to invest the necessary time and effort.

~ **Look At It From Their Perspective.** Andrew Bromley of Ingram, one of the foremost publishing services and distributors, recommends you ask yourself the following questions before approaching a bookstore:

1. Why should a bookshop stock my book when they have limited space and a selection of millions in the market at 60% terms. Why do I/does my book stand out?

2. What margins am I prepared to give away (should I sell 1000 at 30% margin, or 2000 at 60% margin). Is it about money, or exposure for me, or both?

3. Is my book likely to get some PR? Will the press or book media write a review or give it some feature coverage? For example something controversial about it has links to something/somebody famous or changes our views on a famous event etc.

4. How else can I drive demand (book signings, blogs, issue free chapters, book prizes, themed events, radio interviews?

5. Have I sorted distribution?

Distribution

Assuming that your book is good enough to sit well on the shelves of a bricks-and-mortar store, now consider how you will get it there. If you have already arranged for your book to be listed by one of the major distributors used by bookshops, well and good. If not, you may find the practicalities and costs may be prohibitive, so make sure the game is worth the candle.

You will also need to bear the cost of returns: bookstores always expect to buy on a sale-or-return basis. Careful management and substantial confidence in your work is required to avoid ending up at a loss. "To get distribution through bookshops, it has to be more than author footwork," says Lucy McCarrarher of ReThink Press. "If you are a publisher, you can have an account with international wholesalers like Ingram, Bertram, Gardners, Nielsen or Barnes and Noble, where you list all your titles. You can't do this as an individual author.

"The bookstores (worldwide) also have accounts with these wholesalers and that's where they order books from; not direct from publishers or authors – unless a local store does a friendly deal with a local author. So if you are an indie author you have no chance of getting your book into more bookstores because you are not listed with the wholesaler."

It's a matter of those two old business chestnuts: convenience and cost, says Andy Bromley.

Bookshops will buy a) where they can get the book most cheaply, with best margins for them or b) where it's easiest to order. They don't want to bother with individual authors, or even small to medium publishers, hence why they go to a distributor. Ingram supplies distributors like Gardners and Bertram. If you want to 'go global' you need to plug in with somebody who has global reach and can supply a bookstore with stock.

Andy Bromley, Marketing Manager, Ingram.

If unable to order via its usual wholesaler, the bookstore will expect its financial arrangements with you to be the same as those with any of its trade publisher partners: on a sale-or-return basis, and with next-day delivery in response to special orders. In every sale, they will expect to retain a handsome cut of the cover price, typically 40%. Don't expect them to buy your books by the case, because their storage space will be limited. Two or three copies at a time is not unusual. If they buy half a dozen, you have cause to celebrate.

After your initial delivery, it needs to be easy for them to buy more copies of your book – and to return them to you at no cost if they remain on the shelves unsold. The probable answer is that you will have to make a personal trip to the store.

Bookstore chains will expect you to be able to supply copies of your book to ALL their stores, which may run into thousands of books, all printed at your expense. The scale of this upfront investment would preclude most indie authors on financial grounds or at least makes a contract with a major bookstore seem less attractive. [And] the author needs to be wary about the returns issue. That would be fine for the occasional return, but could turn into an economic nightmare with multiple copies. Imagine if 100 bookshops all order 15 print copies on sale-or-return. The returns could wipe out your profits big time!
Helen Hart, SilverWood Books.

Distribution services are starting to become available to self-published authors, but at a substantial cost: for example, IndieReader's new IRIS service charges $395 to add a new book to the IRIS catalogue. You'll need to sell a lot of books to recoup that outlay.

After taking all of these factors into account, you may decide that having your book stocked in bricks-and-mortar bookstores is not quite as alluring as you first thought. There's no shame in that: only a tiny fraction of trade-published books are stocked in each bookstore at any given time.

Think hard and objectively before making a commitment, and if you decide in the end to reject their offer, on your own terms, that's fine. The freedom to choose is one of the joys of being a self-published author.

How to Make Your In-store Pitch

If, after reading all of these cautions, you are still sold on the idea of getting your book stocked in independent bookstores, or just your local branches of a national chain, prepare your approach with the strategy and precision of a military campaign. Keep a clear head. Timing is everything.

In your enthusiasm, don't rush into the store before you have a print book ready to show them, and provide objective evidence to back up your claims for its worth: local media coverage, early reviews, endorsements from appropriate authorities.

Then follow these steps:

- Pick the right store for your book, local to you and/or with a relevant specialist slant.

- Get to know your target bookstore. Visit often, at all times of day.

- Identify the book's official buyer.

- Make an appointment at a time convenient to the buyer; if it's not so convenient for you, too bad.

- Adopt the right tone: polite, professional, respectful. Smile.

- Present an impassioned – but rational – pitch for your book to be sold in that particular shop.

- Provide professional materials in support: a book information sheet, copies of reviews, bookmarks, flyers and business cards showing your author website URL, your social media sites, and any other relevant items.

- Demonstrate how stocking your book will benefit the store – how you will generate new customers (local fans, local interest, local media coverage, your online author platform, your social media activity, etc.).

- If the buyer doesn't make an immediate decision, show your own faith in your product by leaving a complimentary copy of the book for them to examine at their leisure.

- Thank them for their time and leave promptly when you have finished your proposal.

- Don't hassle them for a response – there may be many factors affecting their decision that you don't know about.

- If you haven't heard anything from them after a week, put in a polite call or email, and await their reply.

- If the answer is a "no", don't go back to collect your sample book, unless they ask you to – leave it with them in case they change their mind.

In all of these dealings, respect your contact's professional skill and judgement. It is disappointing to have your book rejected, particularly by a store that you use regularly or which has a special significance for your book – and especially if you know that it has been more receptive to other indie authors. Treat that as good news, by the way – it's far more hopeful for you long-term than if the shop has a blanket policy to reject self-published books.

They know their store and their customer base better than you ever will. If they remain unconvinced, accept their judgement with good grace. Try not to show disappointment or displeasure, and do not take it personally. You may want to return, later, with the same or a different book, to pitch again, so ensure that you accept their decision with good grace.

If you believe they have made a mistake in rejecting your book, there is only one way to make them make a different decision another time: get back out there and sell your books elsewhere and return another time with your next book, a better track record and an undaunted spirit.

In-Store Events

Assuming that you have successfully arranged for your book to be stocked in the store of your choice, try raising your game by offering author events. These need not only be launch events – book signings, readings, demonstrations or activities on appropriate occasions may all be considered, if they offer a clear benefit to the bookstore, i.e. more customers, more sales, and more profit for the store.

Do not assume that any store will welcome a launch event by a debut, unknown, self-published author, any more than they would a debut, unknown trade-published author – but if your first book has sold very well and you're about to bring out a much-heralded sequel, you may see the money signs in the store's buyer's eyes.

Incidentally, bear in mind that any bookshop hosting an in-store event for you will expect sales made to go through their tills and to gain their usual slice of your profit. Don't turn up with a box of books from your own stock and a petty cash tin, assuming you can bypass their system. Nor should you expect bookstore staff to treat you like a celebrity, unless you are confident that you'll generate a mile-long queue of customers outside their door before they open. Be grateful for whatever exposure they offer you, and go in well equipped and mentally prepared to actively engage with customers, without harassing them.

Take props to provide a talking point: military thriller writer Harvey Black brings a dummy of a man in uniform to sit beside him. A bowl of sweets to share on your signing table is literally a sweetener. If you have original illustrations or any other interesting source material, display them to encourage conversation and extend dwell-time at your table.

Above all, be generous with your time and make every customer feel like a million dollars. Great feedback from happy customers, to whose book purchases you've added immeasurable value with special conversations and inscriptions, will persuade the bookstore to continue to support you and to invite you back for more.

Inspiring Successes

Many self-published authors have struck up excellent relationships by following the professional codes outlined above.

The first time I (Dan) went into a bookstore to ask if they'd be prepared to let me do a reading, I was more terrified than I would have been heading to the headmaster's office with the guilty chalk-marks still on my fingers. Like agents, I imagined they were approached constantly, had prepared speeches and stern glances ready and waiting to use to bat away interfering upstart authors. At the very least I thought I'd have to find another store to do my regular browsing because I'd be sure to end up on a pasted under-the-counter barred list.

As it turned out, the guy who owns the store – Oxford's The Albion Beatnik – is just a guy who loves books, and quite likes selling them too. There are two important points in that last sentence. First, there are lots of bookshops in Oxford, where I live. There's even one of the most famous in the world, the original Blackwell's, but I write slightly off-beat stuff with lots of musical references whose natural readership is the kind of person who'd go to a rock gig on a Saturday night, or hang out in a seedy jazz café. The Albion Beatnik specialises in books about music, and by and about the Beat Poets.

It's also a fantastic live music and culture venue, with a book café that plays jazz and is regularly open past midnight. So it was an obvious choice if I wanted to reach my readers.

In the three and a half years since that first visit, I have held tens of events there, featuring poets from around Oxford, the UK, and even those visiting from overseas. These events have brought new customers to the store, and the store has brought new readers to my books.

This is the key to independent bookstores and independent authors working together, bringing something to each other. What we need to do, as self-publishers, is make sure that when we approach a bookstore we are clear exactly what we can bring to them.

Such success is not always premeditated. Rich rewards may be gained from opportunism. English novelist Roz Morris reports on the pleasing outcome of a serendipitous meeting in a pub:

A friend invited me to read my work at an event in a pub. It went well and I got talking to someone from a bookshop. They said they happily stocked indie authors' books and offered to stock mine. I had no idea it could be that easy. Emboldened, I decided I'd approach the two independent bookshops in my part of London.

I didn't ask 'do you stock self-published authors?' Although I wanted to be up front, I thought that might come across as defensive. Instead I asked, 'Do you stock local authors?' In both shops, I showed my books and I was in. I realised that booksellers understand why authors self-publish.

We simply have to go and say hello.

But then came ... the special shop! The funny thing is, I didn't set out to sell to them at all. Barton's is an indie bookshop in Leatherhead, Surrey, and I sometimes shop there. I wandered into Barton's at Christmas, looking for books that friends and family wouldn't have found from online searching (what bookshops do best!). I chatted to the owner, Peter Snell, and we scooted around the shelves, hunting for treasure. I noticed he had a lot of books I already owned, so I'd say 'have you got anything like this?' or 'what do you think of that?'.

Once I'd gathered a stack, I asked if he had any writing books, and then had to explain why I'd read everything he had. That led – without the slightest premeditation – to him looking me up and taking a fancy to my novel. I gave him a copy and the next time I went in, he'd read it not just once but twice – and said he wanted a word about my bizarre imagination.

Now, when I drop in, he finds a way to mention to another customer that I have this rather interesting novel with a snazzy red piano on the cover. The locals are usually impressed that they've met a real, live author and there's another sale! Barton's has been more than usually supportive of my work. They invited me for a signing, want me to do another when my next novel is ready, and my titles are displayed in a prominent position by the till.

Remember, too, what independent bookstores want. They want an eclectic stock so that they are a boutique alternative to supermarkets and Waterstones. Booksellers want to know about exciting, convention-bending work. And who's providing that? Indie authors."

Roz Morris.

These examples demonstrate the natural synergy of free-thinking, independent bookstores with self-published authors. There are impressive success stories in chain-stores too, although it is more difficult to gain a foothold in big chains, where you have to win over not only the local book buyer or store manager, but also conform to corporate policy from head office. But there are also benefits. Store managers within a chain will talk to each other, enjoying a bit of rivalry and also sharing best practice. If one has a good experience of a local self-published author, he may well recommend that author to his nearest neighbouring store.

French resident Alison Morton maintains many friends and former colleagues in her former home town of Tunbridge Wells, England. Careful negotiation, meticulous planning, professional presentation standards, and the guarantee of a large local audience of known supporters, as well as extensive before-and-after event publicity, have helped her to develop a strong relationship with the Tunbridge Wells branch of Waterstones, a leading British chain of booksellers, where she now holds launch events for each of her new novels. She also works effectively with bookstores local to her home in France.

Children's author Karen Inglis has achieved distribution in ten branches of Waterstones through word-of-mouth recommendation from local branches with whom she'd developed a rapport. While a local manager may not be allowed to order your book directly, she advises, they will have the power to recommend you to the central buyer if they think you have a quality product. Establishing your brand via a website is therefore very helpful, as it will enable managers to pass on your links. Karen shares her own sales history in more detail on her website here: http://kareninglis.wordpress.com/marketing-tips/

Any trade-published author and any bricks-and-mortar bookstore, whether indie or in a chain, would be proud to be a part of such success stories.

Supermarkets, Superstores and Other Retail Outlets

Of course, bookstores are not the only bricks-and-mortar shops in which readers buy books. Specialist stores often sell books, and supermarkets and superstores have now entered the fray. US novelist Karen Myers reports on the effectiveness of special interest stores relevant to the themes of her books:

My first series of books is not just regional (Virginia, USA) but also topical (foxhunting). It was straightforward to hit regional non-book-

store booksellers individually, the sort of people that supply horse and foxhunting enthusiasts, and also carry books. They've done very well for me.

Karen Myers

Many authors may find new outlets through this kind of lateral thinking.

Sadly, there is no real potential for self-published books in supermarkets and superstores, whose entry into book retaining has been very selective. They are interested only in offering their customers a very restricted list of bestsellers, often printed in special cut-price editions exclusively for the supermarket shelf, demanding different covers tailor-made for their stores. As with their other product lines, these vast traders call the shots on price, paring the publisher's profit to the bone. No matter how well you think your book would match the customer profile of a particular supermarket chain, you are highly unlikely to secure a worthwhile deal.

It's worth bearing in mind that profit may not be the sole attraction for trade publishers to get their books in supermarkets. Exposure to the millions of shoppers passing through their doors each week will also be of value, particularly if the books currently on promotion in-store are by a prolific author with an extensive backlist available only at full price elsewhere. Supermarket book offers may therefore serve as loss leaders for top-selling authors. Self-published authors should steer a wide berth for now.

Remainder Outlets

Think of remainder outlets as the places where unsold books go to die. These stores get their stock from publishers' stock that boomerangs back from bookstore chains who bought sale-or-return. After shipping both ways, and sitting on a shelf for months, to the trained eye they are not considered fit for resale at full price. They are let go, to cover their costs, via remainder outlets.

If that sounds a sad ending for the hard work of a trade-published author, that's not the worst potential outcome: trade publishers are also unhesitating pulpers. At least as a self-published author, you're unlikely to need to destroy your slow-selling books to create warehouse space for newcomers and rivals and having a spare bedroom stacked high with boxes of unsold books doesn't feel so bad.

If you really need to reclaim your house-space, consider selling them at car boot sales or using them for charitable purposes, unless too many copies have already found their own way down that route. Take heart, says successful American novelist Christine Nolfi, and know that for most indie authors, the real breakthrough to the big time will come not from bookstores at all, but from online retailing:

My books are mainstream women's fiction – the sort of thing bookstores prefer to stock – but I have no experience of getting into such venues. Early in my indie career, several successful authors advised me to focus on ebook sales if I wanted to earn a living. Approaching bookstores directly is an accounting nightmare.

Christine Nolfi, bestselling US Author.

Online Bookstores

In online retailing sites, there is less room for prejudice against self-published authors, largely because most customers neither notice nor care how a book is published. Their interest is essentially in whether this book is their idea of a good read. So online retailing offers a much more even playing field on which the referee is the reader.

As in bricks-and-mortar bookstores, though, you need to be a professional player and ensure that In December 2013, a Guardian feature about the growing dominance of self-published ebooks in the Kindle charts provided the following summary of the even-handedness to publishers shown by Amazon, the leading online producer and distributor of self-published authors' books: "Amazon has been careful not to ghettoise self-published works, instead listing them with equal ranking alongside those from traditional houses, in a move that has irked some established publishers and led to calls for self-published works to be categorised separately."

The articles goes on to quote Richard Mollet, chief executive of the UK Publishers' Association: "publishing companies still offer authors unparalleled creative, financial and marketing support and expertise, helping the author and the work achieve their full potential." This seems a rather petulant and defensive response in the face of such clear evidence to the contrary. Just asserting it doesn't make it so.

To sell well online, though, it is essential that your book is attractive editorially and visually. All of this is well within the self-published author's power, as so many ALLi members ably demonstrate.

Promotional Space

Although there are opportunities for high-spend book promotions on online retail sites (and plenty of online book promotion websites and services beyond the stores themselves, such as bookbub.com), the basic display space allocated to every book will be the same size and in the same format, whether it's the latest *New York Times* bestseller sensation, or a book with no further readership likely than the author's own family and friends.

The visibility of your particular display space will of course vary according to the sales you make, thanks to the algorithms dictating that bestsellers are frequently recommended in "You Might Also Like" listings, but at least you have the same opportunity as any trade-published author to ensure your book is displayed to best effect. In fact, self-published authors have a clear advantage over trade-published authors, because they have control of their own book's profile. If you personally loaded your book onto Kobo, for example, it's very straight forward, and a moment's work, to tweak your book's online blurb, adding in the latest endorsement or tweaking the price to make it fare better in the current marketplace.

Trade-published authors do not have direct access themselves, but are dependent on their publisher's marketing team, whose priorities may lie elsewhere or be focused on the big money-spinning authors. For most books, the trade publisher is unlikely to give the same amount of time and trouble as the average self-published author to developing and updating online book data pages once the book has been launched.

To optimize your chance of sales online, pay careful attention to these core items of your book's online listing:

- Book Metadata

- Book Categories.

- Enticing Book description, appealingly laid out and Search Engine Optimised, again aiding the reader to find it easily through Google and Amazon search engines.

- An appealing author profile, driving readers to your back catalogue, website and social media pages.

The Importance of the Cover Thumbnail

Although with ebooks, there are no spines or back cover to consider, nor choice of finish for the cover stock (which will not show up on the low resolution of the computer screen), the external appearance of the book is critical. The cover must be eye-catching, professional, legible (title and author name), and suitable for its genre. Typically appearing alongside at least half a dozen other book covers, yours should hold its own and draw in the reader to find out more.

Ebook Interior

The interior should be carefully formatted to be easily legible on every kind of e-reader on which it may be read. Just as for print books, it should be error-free, correctly laid out and thoroughly proofread to ensure it's free of typos, misplaced line breaks, unexpected blank pages, and irritating widows and orphans. If not, it won't be just the bookstore proprietor who is on the receiving end of a reader's complaints – they will be there for the world to see, forever, on the review pages of the online retail site.

Once you have met all of these criteria, you are on an even footing with trade-published authors. Sales then depend on the various online retailers' algorithms, which work not on the basis of who has published your book, but on how closely it matches the needs and wants of its customers. Personal bookseller's whims or likes are not the decider here: it's strictly down to scientific calculation via predetermined algorithms.

The exact workings of these algorithms are a closely-guarded secret, but it's safe to assume that one important factor in determining how high your book will come in any customer search within any online bookstore's website is the number and quality of reviews that readers have left against your book.

On that note, we will now turn our attention to the challenge of gaining reviews, both online and elsewhere.

5. Reviews, Reviewers & Book Blogs

TEN YEARS AGO, if you asked an author or publisher about gaining book reviews, they would most likely have answered you in terms of traditional print media – *Publishers' Weekly*, *The Bookseller*, *Times Literary Supplement* or the literary supplements in the daily and weekend newspapers, radio and — to a much lesser extent — TV.

These days, any discussion of book reviews is more likely to summon up a mental image of a screenshot, whether on Amazon, Goodreads, Kobo or any number of blogs. Why has this shift occurred?

Why Online Reviews Matter

There are many good reasons why online book reviews have become front-of-mind.

- They are accessible and democratic – anyone with an online book-buying habit and account may post a review.

- They are controversial, especially since the so-called sockpuppet scandal in 2012, when it was revealed that certain authors and their publishers were trashing their rivals by posting fake, negative reviews.

- They are greatly valued by any author because more online reviews equal greater visibility within the online stores' search engines.

- They are very public, posted for all the world to see.

- They are permanent, unlike a review in a Sunday supplement, which will not linger long beyond the paper's publication date.

- But do trade-published and self-published authors have equal chances of gaining online reviews?

How To Gain Online Reviews

A trade publisher may work hard to gain new reviews for their book of the moment, engineering marketing campaigns and competitions to encourage new readers to review online. They may be able to commit a bigger marketing budget and have more established channels through which to encourage reviews, but they have no more power than the self-published author to ensure that customer reviews are published within online bookstores, and ultimately the decision lies with the reader.

It therefore follows that the best way to get more online reviews is to: (a) publish the best books that you can; and (b) build strong relationships with readers to motivate them to root for you in whatever way they can, not only to buy every book you write, but also to post reviews and make word-of-mouth recommendations.

This book is not the place to expound on the virtues of building an author platform, but it is relevant to mention here the notion of encouraging readers to post online reviews.

Make it your mission to motivate your readers to respond with a review. Do not miss a trick. It will not cost you any money. Most ethical authors would in any case reject the idea of paying for reviews. All it will cost you is lateral thinking and a little application, a positive attitude, and a determined approach. These tools are within the reach of all authors, no matter how they publish their books.

Who Dares, Wins

The first point is simple: ask. Catch your reader's attention at the time when he or she is most receptive to a request to post a review, i.e. when they have just finished reading your book. Include at the end of every book a simple, polite request outlining that you would be very grateful for their feedback online. This is particularly easy for ebooks, where you may include an embedded link in the back matter of your book to take the reader straight to the reviews page on Amazon, Kobo, Nook or wherever else they may have acquired this particular edition.

Many readers are not aware how grateful authors are for online reviews – and why should they be expected to know this? Their lives, unlike yours, are not daily engrossed in the world of publishing and bookselling. However, if they've enjoyed your book, they will almost certainly feel some gratitude towards you and will feel glad of being able to interact with you in this way.

Not all readers are confident writers, and for many, the prospect of writing a book review will fill them with horror and nervous memories of schoolroom challenges and failures. Phrase your request such that it is clear that you are not asking for an academic, literary appraisal, just a few words that reflect their personal appreciation. (Amazon's minimum word count for a book review is a mere 20 words.) Encourage them, make the task easy, and thank them!

Make It Easy

Change the message according to the store in which you are selling your ebook: upload a slightly different edition appropriate to each online store. For example, link to Kobo in the version you sell in the Kobo store, Amazon in Amazon, and so on. By the way, if selling via Amazon, you may consider reminding the reader that there are different Amazon territories, each carrying separate review sites, but it's unrealistic to expect a reader to post their review worldwide in all the different geographical areas which they might not even realise exist. It's usually only other writers who are savvy enough to post their reviews on the same site across multiple territories. Therefore, at the end of a print book, you might consider listing all the online sites on which you'd welcome a review, so that they may take their pick.

Avoid This Pitfall

A cautionary note here on one particular means that some self-published authors have used to try to attract more sales and online reviews: the optional free promotion for a set period allowed by Amazon's KDP Select service. This encourages readers who might not normally buy your book to download it at no cost. The additional downloads may help to boost your book's sales rank, at least temporarily (although the algorithm appears now to have changed, giving much less weight than before to free downloads than to paid sales), but it's a calculated risk: bad reviews are more likely from readers who are disappointed with their freebie because it doesn't match their normal reading choice. Sometimes, on the reviewing front, less is more: better to have a ten 5* reviews than 50 single-star ratings!

Invite Top Reviewers

Another tactic equally open to self-published and trade-published authors is to identify and approach top Amazon reviewers with an invitation to receive a free copy of your book in return for an honest review. As a high-ranking reviewer on Amazon UK, I (Debbie) am approached two or three times a week by authors offering me their books, and these are almost always self-published authors.

From where I'm standing, it seems to me that trade publishers are missing a trick here, and the self-publishers are showing more initiative and bravado, although they aren't always entirely professional in their approach — for example, the one who recently told me she 'expected' a review if she was going to gift me an e-copy of her new full-length novel, which had only one previous review by someone with the same surname and a retail value of just 99p. I was not flattered that she apparently valued my time at around 20p per hour. Just as any trade publishing company might do, trawl through the list of the top reviewers who read books in the relevant genre and approach them with a polite, professional offer. Before approaching them, read their public profile to check whether they welcome such offers – there's no point in wasting your time any more than theirs if they have closed their list. Generally, if a reviewer has made their email address publicly available, it means they're willing to be approached. However, do not assume that you have a right to their time, any more than you have a right to a spot on a bookshop's shelf, simply by dint of having published a book.

In general, book reviewers make no financial gain from their activity, unless perhaps a tiny amount from posting affiliate marketing links to the books that they have reviewed on their website. They do it purely for personal satisfaction. If they review your book, they are doing you a huge favour, giving up usually around three or four hours to read your book and perhaps another hour to write a thoughtful and considered review.

Actively approaching a reviewer in this way is considered perfectly ethical and acceptable behaviour by Amazon, reviewers and readers alike. Just as when approaching a bookshop, you should behave professionally, openly and helpfully, making a great case for why this particular person should read and review your book, and patiently await their response. Do not pressure them or impose a deadline, and if they review your book, whatever they say, thank them politely.

For more insight into this area of activity, where so many self-published authors fear to tread – or tread awkwardly and come away jaded by their experience – read this interview with ALLi author Theo Rogers' about Amazon reviewers: http://selfpublishingadvice.org/blog/why-indie-authors-need-to-understand-the-subculture-of-amazon-reviewers/.

Spread the Word

When you receive a great review, spread the word via social media. Tweet a link, post it on Facebook or Google+, or whichever site you prefer, to hint to other readers that they may like to follow suit. Success breeds success.

Equally, when you receive a bad review, don't respond. Rather than get caught up in a slanging match, no matter how ridiculous or undeserved the review, rise above it and remain professional. Responding with a defensive retort or rallying of your friends to defend your book on your behalf is the hallmark of an inexperienced author who does not understand the etiquette of the marketplace. Keep your gaze high and disregard any slight.

If the poor review is truly unjust and undeserved, discerning readers will in any case be able to spot its flaws without any assistance, just as most people can see straight through gushing praise of a book written by the author's best friend.

You have little control over reviews posted online, other than to request removal of any that are defamatory or clearly inappropriate. If, for example, it's clear the reviewer hasn't read the book but is complaining about a delivery delay or other grievance, or offensive. Concentrate on the positive.

There are ways in which you can make these reviews work harder for you, however your book is published. Firstly, there currently exists (though they may not remain forever) the option on Amazon to vote a review helpful or unhelpful. Some marketers advise you to rally your friends and supporters to vote more favourable reviews helpful, so that the less favourable reviews are pushed down the page, keeping the best ones at the top. Whether you do this or not is down to your own conscience.

Quote favourable reviews in your marketing materials, on your author website or as endorsements on future publications. They are also very useful when promoting your book elsewhere (for example, trying to get it stocked in a bricks-and-mortar store, as discussed in the previous chapter). Even though discerning people will recognise that all reviews are highly objective, it's certainly helpful to be able to cite plenty of online stars.

Engage with Goodreads

As an author, however you are published, there exist excellent, free opportunities to engage with social media specific to readers, such as Goodreads. Many authors swear by Goodreads as a great place for writers to bond with readers, sharing book recommendations and discussions. It's yet another place to solicit reviews.

If you are an ALLi member, you may also join the ALLi group there, which provides authors with the facility to openly invite reviews from other members or indeed to offer to review other members' books. It doesn't have to be a straight swap between authors, if that makes you feel uncomfortable, but it is potentially a useful extra source of new and thoughtful reviews from people you can trust.

Book Blogs

Of course, online retail websites and social networks are not the only source of book reviews. Book bloggers are increasingly influential as trusted sources of recommendations for readers. These may be run by individuals who enjoy reading and reviewing (and sometimes gaining financial rewards via affiliate links promoting the books they review) or by groups with a specific purpose, such as quality assurance sites.

A growing number of readers follow book bloggers who match their own particular tastes and interests as a simple way of finding new books that they are likely to enjoy. Book blogs, second only to trusted friends with similar tastes, are the source of much new reading. In fact, and this is their major strength, many come to see them as trust friends with similar tastes. They wield considerable power.

They often find themselves sinking under the weight of advance review copies (ARCs) from publishers who recognize that because of their specialist readership, they can often be more effective than the book's pages at reaching specific audiences. But book blogs have also been the subject of controversy. The claim by the chair of the 2012 Book Prize judges, Peter Stothard, that self-publishers were lowering the standard of literature sparked outrage. But it was the book blogging community itself that caused the biggest storm. The influence they have over loyal readers means that for self-publishing writers they are a potentially invaluable resource, a way of connecting directly with eager readers.

The better and more influential a book blogger, the more likely they are to be busy. Some book bloggers choose to reduce their load by refusing to review self-published books. Their situation is analogous to that of the bookstore proprietor: they recognise trade publishers as a seal of approval and quality control, and if they have to reduce their to-read pile, that's one easy way to do so.

In 2012, the author of the highly influential *Gav Reads* blog announced explicitly that this was his decision and gave the following reasons:

- We don't know who you are.

- We don't know how you'll react.

- We'll feel guilty when we don't read it.

- We know you're not going to generate hits.

- We don't read cute bunny love stories set in Ancient Rome.

- We know it's going to be rubbish.

Not all book bloggers will be so explicit nor feel so strongly, especially if they have had good experiences of self-published books in the past. However, any self-published author who is pitching a book to a blogger would be well advised to anticipate and subvert these potential objections.

Mainstream Media Reviews

Even with the high profile and volume of online reviews and book blogs, where all kinds of authors meet on a relatively equal footing, many self-published authors desire the more traditional kind of review in mainstream cultural media.

There is no doubt that 2012 was a breakthrough year for mainstream media coverage of self-published authors. 2011 saw interested columns on the stories of John Locke's and Amanda Hocking's success stories, but in 2012, that coverage started, in the very smallest way, to cross into the review columns. Two books that crossed over from self-publishing to the mainstream (to both commercial and critical acclaim), Hugh Howey's *Wool* and Sergio de le Pava's *A Naked Singularity*, helped fly the flag.

And of course, at the commercial rather than literary end of the spectrum, 2012 will forever be the year of that other crossover phenomenon, *Fifty Shades of Gray*. Another key moment was legendary sharp-penned critic Michiko Kakutani's (favourable) review of Art Sepinwall's *The Future Was Televised* in the New York Times.

These pieces have shown that self-published books can hold their own on the review pages – and attract mass sales and readership. It's an encouraging indicator that these high-profile platforms are starting to look less at where books come from and simply at what lies between their covers.

However, mainstream book pages will, like the bloggers, be inundated with ARCs and appeals from trade publishing houses who are also likely to be big-budget advertisers in the paper and therefore have great clout. The self-published author, on such a small budget that he has to think twice about whether he can even afford to dispatch a complimentary copy of his book, simply cannot compete. (By the way, never, ever send a free review copy unless it has specifically been requested – it will almost certainly be disposed of unread.)

Alternative Editorial

Although it's disheartening for the self-published author to feel powerless in that particular sphere, there is no need to despair: book review pages are not the only means by which to gain mainstream coverage of a book. Delve beyond the "books" or "arts" or "culture" sections of any major paper to find the feature pages, the editorial and talking point sections of the newspapers. Here are opportunities to connect with a much wider range of readers. When a book makes this crossover, readers of the article stop thinking about a book simply as a book and start seeing it as essential further reading about questions that are central to their lives.

This approach works particularly well for the high concept book, and the book with an unusual theme or approach, such as *One Day, Room, Chavs* or *We Need to Talk About Kevin*.

Self-published books, being free of the bounds and conservatism of trade publishing houses, might be seen as the natural home of more thought-provoking topics, and might therefore be the first place that editors would be advised to look for such material.

Editors may not realise this yet – so the self-published author with a story to tell and an unusual angle to offer should actively seek opportunities to present their book to the appropriate section editor with the news angle or feature idea clearly spelled out.

Start Small

Another inroad is to start by aiming closer to home, gaining coverage and a reputation with regional media, print, TV or, more likely, radio, where there is an ongoing need for locally available commentators and experts, and generally a much smaller staff than on national media. Approaching your local paper or lifestyle magazine is generally more affordable and practical for the self-published author than competing for the top national spots – and may also translate into higher sales and readership of your book, because local audiences tend to feel more ownership and connectivity.

Gaining a local reputation helps build clips, collateral and credibility for approaching national media further down the line.

To increase your chance of having your book accepted for a review, blog or media feature , always include in your application:

- Your credentials as a high quality author, For example, author website, previous media coverage, awards, bestsellers and so on.

- Existing positive reviews.

- Evidence of how you will drive traffic to the blog or review outlet. For example, your social media following.

- A professional quality information sheet about your book, giving title, jacket and other important metadata, a summary and any review quotes or author information that's relevant.

Another potentially important player in raising your profile and so reach new readers is the library system. The next chapter will help you play your (library) card right for maximum benefit.

6. Libraries

OF ALL THE segments of book trade examined by this book, the library sector is, anecdotally, the most encouraging of the self-publishing author. Librarians love books and most of them love writers too. Most are very sympathetic to authors, some are even authors themselves. If a writer can demonstrate a good track record, and demand for a book, an acquiring librarian will generally give it a fair hearing.

More than one-tenth of publishers' net book sales are to libraries so there is undoubtedly scope here for the author-publisher too. A search of WorldCat, the outer facing catalogue of the library system, reveals titles published by KDP, Smashwords, Createspace and Ingram (Lightning Source & IngramSpark) are all available in libraries — so some librarians are clearly buying self-published books that fit their acquisitions guidelines.

Unlike bookstores, where purchases are often dictated by a head office, libraries operate independently of each other. Each library operates its own policy, and stock is either ordered from catalogues (such as the Bookseller) or by its chosen book supplier based on its community profile. Each library has its own budget and can spend it how they want, within broad parameters.

How Libraries Work

It's easy to obtain a list of libraries through your country's Library Association. You need to recognise that there are four kinds of library — public, academic, school, and special, and each has a different purpose and orders different kinds of books.

- **Public Libraries:** Government funded local and national libraries that serve the general public

- **Academic Libraries:** The college and university library market, which, although relatively smaller, usually has more money the public sector to spend on books

- **School Libraries: Although with a smaller budget than** public or academic libraries, important for children's or young adult writers.

- **Special libraries: i.e.** libraries devoted to specific purposes e.g medical, law, corporate, usually privately run, with budgets from tiny to huge, and – significant for niche writers in those sectors

The book world has developed a system to serve the special needs of librarians, and in most countries, libraries have their own, tailor-made distribution companies which accommodate trade publishers. Understanding how this book-buying system works will help you gain a foothold in it.

There are different distributors to consider in different countries, but here's an example of those in the USA:

- Quality Books Inc.: http://www.quality-books.com/

- Unique Books Inc.: http://www.uniquebooksinc.com/

- Baker & Taylor: http://www.baker-taylor.com/ (technically they are a wholesaler but they can also help you access the library market)

- For ebooks: Overdrive.

Libraries will generally buy hardback and trade books and tend to shy away from mass market paperbacks, though there are exceptions. Ebooks are increasingly popular.

The Big Five trade publishers have been ambivalent about ebook lending in libraries, in many cases holding back for fear of the ease of copying and piracy. This leaves more room for self-published authors to get in on the ebook action in libraries.

For romance authors in particular, finding a way into this system can be very worthwhile. Romances are the hottest circulating category of ebooks for public libraries, and authors do not have to be known quantities to get circulated widely. Romance readers are voracious and cannot get enough. but libraries' demand for ebooks in all genres is large and growing, and we need to find a way to meet it. ALLi is in the process of encouraging Overdrive to set up a specific programme for self-published books.

Preparing Your Approach

You can't count on just walking into a library and having them take your book, not even if you're giving it away. Librarians are happy to get the right books for their readers, but they also have constraints on what books they can accept and policies on what they can and cannot buy. The high cost of storage and distribution is a practical limitation, and just as in bookstores, shelf space is limited. As is time. Librarians are busy people with little time to read about new books. So it's up to you to identify which librarians would be most likely to buy your book and how to get them interested.

Librarians need to believe your book is something their readers will want to read. Before you make an approach, have a book information sheet that makes it clear what readership your book is directed at and comparable titles.

As always in terms of drawing attention to your book, being able to produce published book reviews will increase your credibility as an author. Librarians generally rely on vendor lists where self-published authors rarely appear or pre-publication book reviews in trade magazines such as *Publishers Weekly* (USA) and *The Bookseller* (UK) or specific library trade magazines like *Library Journal*, *Booklist*, *CHOICE*, and *Forecast*.

School Library Journal is an offshoot of *Library Journal* that specializes in children's and YA books. There are also review magazines, online plus print, that are specific to genres, like *RT Book Review* (romance) and *Locus Magazine* (science fiction and fantasy). The librarian who is specifically interested in indie books may consult *IndieReader*.

Kirkus and PW Select allow self-publishing authors to pay for a review. This fee (rightly) doesn't guarantee a good review, and neither is it cheap. PW Select is viewed by some librarians as a kind of ghetto, not worth the read.

An alternative to reviews is to run events and build local popularity. Librarians, in the main, like to stock books of local interest, so if you're doing a lot of local events, talks, or speaking gigs, or have some press, TV or radio coming up, let your local libraries know. Alert your library in advance to give them sufficient time to order your book.

These two case studies from ALLi members illustrate the value of a local link:

Overall, the Welsh libraries were well down on my list of possible outlets with regard to selling or even stocking my books. I had no idea how it might work and it was entirely by chance that I walked into my local library and met the head-buyer. We enjoyed an informal, unplanned chat.

I left a couple of paperbacks with her, so she could peruse the actual product. By the time I'd driven home and logged on to my email, there was a request that I supply 48 books, a dozen copies of each title and an invitation to be a guest speaker at Conwy Library on World Book Day.

Of course, the fact that these novels are set in well known Welsh towns and locations has clearly helped my cause, but her very first remark to me was that she loved the covers! Yet more confirmation that people do, judge books by their covers, at least initially. It has been a challenge to design covers that work as thumbnails around the Internet but look equally good transferred to paperback, but this is clearly well worth the time and investment.

Novelist Jan Ruth, writing in Wales

I'm a huge fan of libraries because they fed my endless appetite for new stories when I was an eager reader as a child. I wouldn't be the person I am now, let alone the writer I am, if it weren't for such easy access to so many books. Now I am a writer, I wanted to give something back. Both of my novels are set in Birmingham and, because the setting is integral to each story, I'm eager for the books to reach as many "Brummies" as possible. I got in touch with the reader development team for Birmingham Libraries and asked if I could tell them about my books. The reception I got was brilliant. My details went to all the community libraries and I suddenly found I had a book tour in place! Some library visits were to speak to an existing group, others were specially arranged author events. In all cases I was made extremely welcome by the library staff and met by a group of interested people. Sometimes it was an intimate chat with a small group of readers, other times I spoke for longer to a larger audience. Every time was great fun. Not only did I meet people who were interested in my books – either having read the library copy or keen to buy one from me – but I also got to interact with avid readers and pick their brains about what kind of stories they enjoy, what kind they'd like to read. I'm looking forward to the visits I still have lined up and hope Birmingham libraries will be interested in my next book so I can visit again when it's out.

English writer Katharine D'Souza

Once you've made initial sales to a few local libraries, it is much easier to sell to others and to different kinds of libraries too, so don't stop at your first success story. Expand your territory.

One small practical detail: ensure your book has an ISBN. Without it, as far as the library system is concerned, your book doesn't exist.

Making Your Approach

To make the most of the opportunities libraries offer, now and in the future, nothing is more important than making the librarians aware of your book and its merits. Dust down your library card, stop by and introduce yourself. The librarian who purchases books is usually called the Acquisitions Librarian or the person in charge of Collection Development. Sometimes there are more than one, each with responsibilities for particular categories. The person who acquires travel books, for example, may be different from the person who acquires literature or genre fiction.

Check the website. If your book is a children's book, the person you want is likely to be Head of the Children's Department or of Youth Services. Each library may have a collection development policy that gives a broad outline of what they collect and whether they buy it or have it donated.

Discover what the library buys, and talk to the librarians about how they make purchases, their time-frames and so on. As in bookshops, build relationships. Some libraries have special systems or sections specifically for self-published local authors.

As always, be polite, professional, and respectful. Call, email, or set up a brief meeting to ask about donating some copies of your books. Yes, donating. Libraries are usually non-profit organisations and at the moment are under funding pressure. They like — and need — donations, so in most cases you'll need to be willing to donate.

A lot of libraries prefer two copies or more. Cataloging even a fiction book takes time and effort, and many libraries find it makes more economic sense to have at least two copies.

If pitching your book doesn't work, ask about staging an event or find another way you can fill a need for them. An event is a great way to get "into" your local library, become acquainted with them and meet your local readers. Many libraries also have reading groups that might love to have you visit as a guest author.

For children's author Karen Inglis , this tactic served as a springboard. "I did a children's event at my local library, which was a good way to get exposure. I recently discovered that one of my books subsequently had 72 library borrows."

Asking others to request your book can get a library to put your book on the shelves. Libraries usually take requests seriously, but they are also well trained in detecting when such requests are genuine. So don't ring up pretending to be a reader. Ask people who have a genuine enthusiasm for your book to make the request.

Once The Book Is Stocked

If your book is borrowed regularly, the librarian may be happy to pay for additional copies. If not, your book may not last. How long a book stays on the shelf depends on the library's available space, how often the book is checked out, but also on the book's condition. Books last longer at central libraries that have a larger and more comprehensive collection, but branches are smaller buildings and their collections are supposed to be popular. That's what they're for, bringing popular books to the general public.

So books, especially novels, tend to be weeded from branch libraries after a year or so if they are not circulating. That's why you sometimes see libraries selling off books that are apparently still in good condition: there simply haven't been enough loans to justify giving them shelf space.

All other things being equal, paperbacks circulate better than hardcovers, and hardcovers with dust-jackets better than hardcovers without.

Is there anything authors can do to improve the chances that our books will be found and checked out more often? As always, your cover art is important. Enticing descriptions on the sides of the dust-jacket, or the front and back of the paperback, will encourage more borrows.

Let the librarians know about all marketing you are doing, including email promotions and in-store events. The library wants to know that the author is equally invested in the book's success.

If your library has any kind of book blog or feature on their website, offer to contribute, or have someone post a review or make a book recommendation. If you have local fans, encourage them to get involved. Urge local social media followers and email-list subscribers to ask about your book next time they are in the library, perhaps offering some kind of incentive.

If you haven't already offered to hold an event before they agreed to stock your book, do so now, whether for the general public or as part of one of their regular book groups or reading groups. "Don't confine yourself to purely promotional events," says Scottish novelist Ali Bacon. "Find out what kind of thing the library would like to provide for users and work out what you could offer to help them. My local council area runs an annual Discover Festival for people to do new things or learn new skills, where I ran a workshop."

Teaming up with other authors to provide a joint event can add appeal to your local library. Ali joined forces with the nine other authors in the writers' cooperative Bristol Women Writers to produce *Unchained*, an anthology of their short stories and poems, published to mark Bristol Central Library's 400th anniversary. Launched as part of the Bristol Literature Festival 2013, it led on to a writing workshop as part of the Bristol 400 programme.

Our group now has a much higher profile, and Bristol Libraries welcome our suggestions for events and activities. It has also given me exposure over a wider area than before and has given all of us enriched network-ing opportunities with other writing groups, publishers, editors and performers. The library tie-in was definitely important in catching at-tention and giving off good vibes – writers and readers all love libraries!

I made the first approach to the libraries, but after a couple of events they started coming to me. I also appeared on local radio during Nation-al Libraries Week as a result of library events and contacts. Although I originally offered free copies of my novel, since then the libraries staging events have usually bought copies of whichever book is being promoted.

Ali Bacon, novelist.

Just like bookstores, librarians are effectively hand-selling books. Think of them as ambassadors for your book, quietly but effectively spreading your words to the wider world. Librarians not only help library members find suitable books, they also discuss with each other what they are reading, and the books they read and recom-mend circulate more.

American businessman Mitchell Davis, founder of BookSurge which was later acquired by Amazon and turned into CreateSpace, now offers the book world a new service, BiblioBoard, "the patron-first, mobile library". Davis believes libraries can reinvent themselves in a new publishing landscape as a useful discovery service.

So far, the patterns of what propels some self-published books to break out have been mostly haphazard. Libraries can change that… [and] help patrons make sense of it all. In the process, they can re-invent themselves in the value chain and provide a critical reader service.

Libraries have struggled to participate in the digital era while stuck in one-book one-user business models established by publishers [but] as curation meets new technology and business models afforded by Biblio-Board, libraries can make available thousands of fantastic eBooks and be adding new titles all the time.

Since this is provided to libraries and patrons as a book discovery service (not a sale of content at typical eBook prices), it will be affordable for all libraries and able to scale to fit any library budget... with no checkouts, returns or multi-user limits. The initiative can go viral and serve millions of patrons without creating wait lists or unchecked demand-driven acquisition spending. Patrons will find books that resonate and they will tell others and this will drive a new readership base for that author.

Mitchell Davis, Literary Entrepreneur

Davis anticipates that soon, in terms of book discovery, "libraries and their patrons will be better at publishing than the big publishers". You can read more on Mitch's ideas at http://pubsmartcon. com/libraries-patrons-can-beat-publishers-publishing/.

Other Ways of Earning Income Within Libraries

If you find the only way to get your book into libraries is to donate copies, do not be downhearted or deterred. There are other ways that you may benefit , financially and otherwise, from having your books stocked there:

- Earnings: Register for Public Lending Rights which accrue from borrows over time

- Exposure: your book is being displayed on equal terms alongside trade-published works (the average borrower will not know the difference)

- Book discovery: borrowers may review and recommend your books, helping you reach more readers.

"I once gave away several dozen of my indie books to public libraries, and my philanthropy was more profitable than I expected," says author-publisher, John Yeoman. "The books contained a last page with a subscription form for my paid newsletter [and] I gained several subscriptions."

"My involvement with libraries has definitely raised my profile locally," says Ali Bacon. "Although audiences were fairly modest, some of the events were covered in local papers which also helped spread the word. One press contact came through my local library. And I was quite thrilled when I registered for PLR and found my novel *A Kettle of Fish* has so far been borrowed over 200 times!"

To be eligible for PLR payments,you will need to register with the appropriate organisation that covers your country's lending system.

Joining your region's Authors' Licensing and Collecting Society (ALCS) is also highly recommended, as this organisation distributes to authors any rights income gained from various uses of published work such as photocopying. Again, the benefit isn't only financial, as novelist Linda Gillard, based in Scotland, explains:

An author's income is usually small and the fees paid out by PLR & ALCS are always welcome. Membership of ALCS and being registered for PLR have both increased my income. But I also appreciate knowing how many people are borrowing my books in libraries. I'm also reassured to know that ALCS - for a lifetime fee of £25 in the UK - will protect and promote the rights of authors writing in all disciplines, ensuring we get fair payment for the various uses of our work.
Linda Gillard, writing in Scotland

Working closely and strategically with your local library can clearly help you raise your profile locally, and then further afield as your reputation spreads.

Another great local opportunity to raise your profile that seems to be on almost everybody's doorstep these days is the literary or cultural festival, which may or may not also involve local libraries. The next chapter will address the growing opportunities for self-published authors to raise their profile alongside trade publishers at festivals.

7. Festivals & Events

FESTIVAL CULTURE IS proliferating throughout the arts. There seems just now to be an endless appetite for literature festivals. Alongside the longest-established, biggest and best-known events, there are more and more small, local and/or niche events springing up, each offering their own unique flavour to provide book-lovers with ever-increasing choice.

All of these festivals have at their centre authors of every variety, from cerebral academic to celebrity autobiographer. Unless they are aiming at a narrow niche or genre, there is often room for both of these, and everything in between. The reader is spoiled for choice.

Keeping Up With The Times

As the profile of self-publishing grows, it seems reasonable that literature festivals should include self-published authors. Many festival organisers are beginning to do this, albeit tentatively. The minimum entry level seems to be the offer to give an information session explaining the concept of this new publishing phenomenon. Including talks about self-publishing is often a commercially sound move for a festival, demonstrating to the audience, and potential sponsors, that a festival is moving with the times, and addressing the latest publishing trends.

Although not as inclusive as inviting self-published authors to join the mainstream event programme, such talks do at least acknowledge their existence and bode well for future developments and collaborations. One would think any festival organiser wishing to remain credible could no more ignore the rise of self-publishing than the proliferation of e-readers. Yet self-published authors are under-represented at literature festivals, or even excluded. Unfortunately, even those organisers with the best intentions towards self-published authors may sometimes come unstuck.

One example is the prestigious Boston Book Festival which, in 2013, promised a new "Indie Alley", dedicating 30 stands specifically to self-published authors. In practice, the result was disappointing, as local author Christine Frost described on the ALLi blog, before sharing some constructive suggestions for better collaboration in future:

Unfortunately, it did not go well. The printed program offered little enlightenment about Indie Alley or its precise location. The venue map showcased traditional publishers and literary organizations in their usual spots. Rather than include Indie Alley in the exhibitor list, it appeared as a pale orange ad toward the back of the program. No signs directed attendees to it. I traversed the perimeter of the festival, eager to see fellow indie authors, and eventually gave up in favour of not missing out on the dozens of readings and panel sessions to choose from.

The Boston Book Festival is comprised of two full-time and one-part-time staff, and relies on a small army of volunteers. I was told the amount of extra effort to coordinate Indie Alley proved to be too much in the face of the increased phone calls and emails in addition to the unhappiness that was felt on all sides of it. Ultimately, I was told, they can't be all things to all people, and independent authors should organize their own event.

I was disappointed that it was deemed such a failure. Lessons were certainly to be had on both sides. Better strategy would have made Indie Alley more visible. The follow-up conversation might have been more constructive, with indies offering more collaborative solutions to perhaps help organize their own space at the event in the future.

While BBF organizers solidly shut down the idea of trying to in-corporate self-published authors again after this experience, I'm hoping that eventually there can be a chance to revisit this to make it a more positive experience for everyone. With ever more authors turning to self-publishing, there is a host of opportunities to showcase the wealth of

talent, innovation, and experience indie authors offer, through exhibits and panel discussions, and there would be plenty of interest among the attendees of this great Boston tradition.
   Christine Frost, US Author.

This is just one example of major literature festival at which the growing and important sector of self-publishing is sidelined or ignored. On reading of Christine Frost's experience at the Boston Book Festival, self-published author Warren Shuman commented: "I am not surprised at your unfortunate experience. I have seen the same sort of ignorance at other book fairs ... These 'once a year' so-called book experts really do not keep up with the huge changes in the digital book world. It's not only bad for us. It's cheating the attendees as well."

The Festival Organiser's Challenges

Clearly, any self-published authors hoping to play a part in literature festivals need to be mindful of the challenges and constraints facing festival organisers, and to accommodate and work around them. Engineering these large and varied events is a complex and stressful job, requiring logistical calculations, extensive year-round publicity, and massive investment. Before considering how self-published authors may get in on their action, it's worth getting some perspective on how festival organisers operate.

Their brief is to secure an appealing programme, to a pre-ordained budget, and to optimise ticket sales against a meticulously timed schedule, while satisfying both sponsors and audiences that they're getting excellent value for money. For festivals that run annually, a model to which most will aspire, each year's programme must be varied, topical, appealing and newsworthy.

The guest authors must be dependable, presentable, entertaining and safe – and sufficiently appealing to the public to sell books in good numbers from the inevitable festival bookshop, usually a pop-up run by local traders, which may be the nearest chain's branch or a local independent, trying to serve hundreds of customers simultaneously and swiftly so that they're on time for their next events.

The festival must also be financially viable. Here is a shopping list of some of the expenses that the organiser will incur:

- Venue hire.

- Audio-visual equipment.

- Public liability insurance.

- Website development and maintenance (probably year round).

- Publicity materials – brochures, posters, paid advertising space, etc.

- Box office costs – staffing, ticket printing and distribution, IT systems,

- Back office staff and administration.

- Cleaning and facilities management.

Quite a list, even before adding fees paid to authors and performers. Even paying staff to man the event may not be feasible. Most of the big ones, like Olympic Games, will depend on an army of volunteers to help them run efficiently.

And those author fees? Don't count on those, even if you're trade published and a household name. Dolores Montenegro, writing in *The New Statesman* in October 2013, reports that not only does Cheltenham, one of the largest and most prestigious festivals in the UK, not offer a fee to many of its guest authors, it doesn't pay their travel or overnight expenses either, saving its budget to fund high-profile celebrities such as sportsmen and rock stars who will help get the event national media attention:

The literary festival of old was based on a communal model. All authors, from Max Hastings to debut novelists, were treated the same. The big authors pulled in the punters and subsidised the smaller writers ...

It was a lovely idea but rarely happens nowadays. Many festivals have a two-tier approach to author care. The big names get limos, love and impeccable organization whereas the smaller names are shunted off into small venues and quietly forgotten about ...

The retort would be that festivals are about raising profiles and selling books. Authors are expected to be paid in book sales, but most novelists I know are lucky if they sell a dozen copies. And it's not just unknown writers: one former Man Booker winner regularly fills 500-seater venues but afterwards might sell just 20 books.

Dolores Montenegro.

Perhaps the biggest challenge facing the festival organiser is that the events all have to be interesting. Not all authors are good at speaking before a live audience, and many books are hard to convey or discuss in such a setting. Booking a big name is only a small part of the job: the events have to be well choreographed and planned to satisfy the audience. It's no wonder that so many festivals plump for dependable audience-pleasers with backgrounds in show-business.

Size Matters

Whereas the larger festivals will have the pulling power to attract substantial sponsorship to help them offset their costs, and the established mailing lists and contacts to be reasonably confident of breaking even or making a profit, many smaller festival organisers have no such security or assurance. Quite a lot are organised by local booksellers trying to draw in extra custom, without the benefit of extra staff or budget to make it happen.

The pivotal role of local bookshops can work to the self-published author's advantage, if he or she has already cultivated a good relationship with their local bookstore. On the other hand, for organisers operating with limited manpower, the prospect of dealing with individual self-published authors presents a much more challenging and time-consuming prospect than liaising with the extensive staff of a trade publishing house. These one-man-bands don't have secretaries or publicity aides to answer phone calls or respond to emails; if the author's out walking the dog when the organiser calls, too bad.

Responding to Christine Frost's article about the Boston Book

Festival, self-published author Maggie Lynch expounds upon this point:

Event planners like to deal with publishers because they have a single point of contact for multiple authors. This makes it more manageable and they deal with someone who understands the ins and outs of event coordination. When dealing with individual authors, they are dealing with 30 different peoples' ideas about how the event should help them and, in effect, trying to get all the information out of those 30 different people.

My suggestion is that if indie authors want to be included in events, they form groups under some name and have a coordinated effort with a single point of contact. That contact person then serves as the voice for the group.

I recently coordinated a successful Kobo/Bookseller event. It was primarily indie authors, though we did have a couple of traditional authors and a few hybrid authors. I personally spent the equivalent of two months' time recruiting participants, making sure every one of the 19 authors was on board, sending information as needed, participating in social media, signing event contracts, planning PR and making sure it went out, coordinating with the bookseller, coordinating with Kobo, etc. I had lots of help with other volunteers at the event, but again someone had to coordinate that. In other words, even with the opportunity to participate it still required a lot of coordination and 'herding' of authors. Like everything in this business, we have to work together and step up and lead, instead of waiting and hoping that we can simply pay a fee and walk in the door and sell. I have always found that group efforts open doors where individuals have more difficulty.

Maggie Lynch, Indie Author.

What Self-Published Authors Can Bring

Self-published authors who are mindful of the festival organisers' challenges and take them into account when making their approach will stand a much greater chance of success in gaining admission on equal terms with their trade-published peers.

It certainly can be done. Enterprising self-published authors are finding creative, appealing ways to enter the fray. The Triskele Books collective of five self-published novelists devised not one, but two, events that were snapped up by the organisers of the 2013 Chorleywood Literature Festival: a panel discussion about the nature of their author collective; and an innovative "Human Reference Library" session, in which each of the five offered one-to-one consultation slots for members of the public interested in discussing different aspects of self-publishing.

Publicised enticingly in the Festival brochure, and energetically by the five authors via their huge combined social media and online presence, both of these events attracted a healthy attendance of writers, aspiring writers and readers, aged from 11 to over 80.

Self-published authors may also gain tangential access to events, in spite of, rather than because of, their self-published status. These opportunities should not be dismissed lightly: they increase the author's chance of being drawn in to the main events' programme in future years — or invited to other events.

There are also opportunities to be associated with the Festival, even if you are not actually a part of its official programme. If there are local radio stations or print media reporting on the event, it's worth pursuing openings there, as both are likely to be searching for related news stories and features.

I (Debbie) recently engineered the opportunity to join a radio discussion panel broadcast live by BBC Radio Gloucestershire from the Authors' Lounge at the Cheltenham Festival, with two trade-published authors, one of whom was Katie Fforde, President of the UK Romantic Novelists' Association. With the focus of the discussion on the changing nature of publishing and reading, this was a valuable opportunity to draw attention to the rising profile of self-publishing before a significant audience.

How The Self-Published Author Should Proceed

Firstly, consider which of the three main areas in which you can add depth and breadth to any literature festival programmes. Which of the following best suits your work, your personality and your experience?

- Acting as a panel member for discussion about self-publishing, an area of increasing interest to many festival visitors, whether writers aspiring to self-publish, or readers keen to understand what self-publishing really means.

- Appearing as a writer, talking about and reading from your books..

- Offering advice or education as an expert, with the ability to lead teaching workshops or seminars. For example, on different aspects of self-publishing or book marketing or based on the content of your book(s).

Also take into consideration what you personally want to get out of appearing at the festival. Raising your author profile, meeting new readers and selling books will probably be high on your list, but you may also be keen to share particular experiences or thoughts, either those that led you to write the book, or ones from your self-publishing journey. And to learn from others.

Each of the three kinds of event listed above offers considerable scope. If you want to talk about self-publishing, for example, on which aspect would you like to focus? The production process, cover design, book marketing, or selling foreign rights? Which subject can you present in the most interesting way?

If you come up with a great talk that is well-received, you may well find yourself asked to give the same talk many times over. That's fabulous, but only if you'll enjoy it as much yourself the twentieth time as the first!

How To Choose The Most Appropriate Festival

Then find a festival that suits you. Different festivals, conferences and events have different focusses. For example, PubSmart in Charleston is very much focussed on the business of books, the kind of entrepreneurial indie author who wants to make a living from writing. They will welcome a quite different kind of proposal than, say, The Literary Conference in London, which has as it focus literary values in a digital age.

Once you've worked out which event you'd like to speak at and what you'd like to deliver, write a letter succinctly explaining why the session you wish to offer is ideal for this particular festival — and why you are the person to deliver it.

- Visit the festival website to enable you to address its specific brief, understand how the festival is organised and how effectively they publicise the events.

- Examine previous programmes to acquire a feel for the type of events they prefer.

- Consider how they describe similar events to get an idea of their audience.

- Connect your skills and interests to theirs in a meaningful way.

Online searching, particularly Twitter and Google, are the best places to find the right festivals. (And don't forget to share your experience via ALLi afterwards, to help others gauge whether it's right for them.)

How To Pitch To Festival Organisers

Compile a submission package that will make your chosen festival organiser want to book you. Rather like a manuscript submission package, this will consist of an all-purpose core of material that you can then adapt to make it specific to other festivals.

Your package should be a single document. You are selling about an hour of your time for a talk, workshop or panel discussion. To do that effectively you need to demonstrate that what you have to say is of interest to festival goers (this is the equivalent of the pitch); that you have enough well-thought-out material to fill an hour (not less and not more – this is the equivalent of the synopsis) and that you are the best person to say this (because when you're speaking direct to an audience, you matter).

With the above in mind, your package should include a pitch of 150-200 words on:

1. what you intend to talk about;

2. what format your talk will take; and

3. why this will be really interesting.

A good way to approach this is to describe it as it might appear in the festival programme, with a single paragraph that will ensure your event is a sell-out.

Then, outline the general areas you intend to cover in the order you intend to cover them. If you envisage doing anything other than a straightforward talk, this is the place to say that. This is important; variations in format can make an event really exciting and be a great selling point but they can also be scary to organisers. If you will be using handouts, for example, state that you have a set of workshop materials that you will bring with you. A good festival will reimburse large photocopying costs, but no-one wants to find an overstretched volunteer to rush around to duplicate them at the last minute.

If they don't know you, they will envisage this being a last-minute thing, however much you tell them otherwise! In my experience as an event organiser (Dan), 90% of writers turn up very nearly late, expecting to find access to a free photocopier, breezily holding a handful of sheets and saying, "Oh, I assumed you'd be able to take care of that."

If, instead, you behave well and make their lives easier, organisers will clamour to have you back.

Avoid slideshows/powerpoint if possible. Laptops and projectors may be everywhere in your day job, but most festivals still struggle to find venues with adequate IT facilities. If your presentation is going to need AV, the organisers will look at their timetable and the number of available slots will instantly shrink. Every event organiser has tales of speakers making assumptions about IT that make them very unwilling to take risks.

If you feel strongly that you need to work that way, discuss it after you've been booked.

Include your press kit with your application. You will be asked for it once you're booked, but it both sells you and shows a degree of professionalism if you offer one up front. The press kit is what the organisers will use along with your pitch to sell your event to the public and the media. It should contain the following:

- A relevant, persuasive bio, ideally in concise but syntactical bullet points that clearly show why you are the best person to give this talk, including previous public speaking experience.

- Any relevant press reviews or references from previous events.

- Website links (to your personal website, rather than your books on retail sites).

- A publicity photo, ideally in high resolution (300dpi+) for print use, and low resolution (72dpi) for the festival website.

Festival Organisers & Self-Publishers: FAQs Answered

How do I find self-published authors who will be the best match for my festival?

If you are looking for events on a certain theme, the chances are you will already be asking around or know who the experts are in that field. Don't be afraid if self-publishers' names come up. Many people choose self-publishing because they have a passion for quirky, niche subjects that can make for the most wonderfully entertaining talks. ALLi is always happy to make suggestions.

How do I know if there's an audience for this? If I don't know who this person is, chances are my audience won't.

Festival- and event-goers fall into two categories: those who go for the person speaking; and those who go for the subject being spoken about. Events divide around those two categories of punter. Obviously some well-known (and less well-known but loved within their niche) authors will sell an event by their name and, yes, self-publishing authors are beginning to fall into this category but not, as yet, in great numbers.

On the other hand, many of the best festival events attract through what they are about. A self-published author's lack of high profile doesn't detract from their ability to give a wonderfully interesting talk that would fit the flavour of your festival perfectly. This is particularly true for workshops.

I am worried about the quality of self-publishing authors' work.

Follow the recommendation sin Chapter Two. And don't be afraid to contact ALLi who will suggest authors we can vouch for and try to help you to find an author who meets your specific requirements, and has experience of speaking at such events (provided your reimbursement to writers is fair and equitable). If ALLi has put you in touch with an author, please provide honest feedback about them and their events, so as to help us serve both authors and festivals more effectively in future. We welcome your feedback whenever you have a self-published author, especially when someone has impressed, so that we can build a large, reliable network of trusted speakers.

Self-published authors can be over-assertive and hands-on. I understand they have to be, because they do everything for themselves but I don't have time to hand-hold and be at the other end of the telephone/email for them all the time.

We have drawn up the list of guidelines for authors at the end of this Chapter. ALLi advises all members seeking a festival booking to read these guidelines.

First, however, we'd like to make some suggestion to festival organisers as to how to ensure you get the best out of self-published authors.

Guidelines for Festival Organisers Programming Self-Publishers

Consider the value that self-publishing writers can bring to your festival. If you have not already planned one, consider holding a panel or workshop session on self-publishing, run by experienced self-published authors.

And consider self-published authors as authors as well as publishers, by which we mean don't forget to invite them to talk about/read from their books or work-in-progress. Many writers self-publish because their books do not match trade publishers' genres or other constraints. This kind of book, and the writers who produce them, can provide much more thought-provoking and entertaining talks than many within the mainstream.

Where authors are doing the same thing at a festival, do treat them the same in terms of their fee for speaking, travel and accommodation, green room access, gala dinners, and other incidentals. Don't have double-standards based on how their books are published or copies they sell or degree of fame.

All writers recognise that festivals depend on big names to attract their audience, but interesting, less well-known authors add breadth and depth, give the festival credibility, and potential for future growth. Paying a flat fee for all speakers, plus a percentage of ticket sales for an event, is an equitable way for organisers to balance all the variables.

Include all participating authors in your festival communications, not only as a courtesy, but also to ensure that they do not need to keep coming back to you for clarification on issues.

Ensure fair coverage in your promotional materials and practices, giving equal space to all authors in the programme and on the website, with equal opportunities to have a web link and photograph featured.

Include your self-published authors in your media campaign, giving them coverage in your press releases and pointing journalists in their direction. Ensure any in-house podcasts, radio broadcasts, and video-casts reflect the diversity of your festival.

If there is a festival bookstore, make sure self-published authors are able to sell through it and given signing times and space, where this is general festival practice.

Event Guidelines for Self-Publishing Authors

If the festival organiser does you the courtesy of treating you on an equal footing with trade published authors, make sure you reciprocate. In particular, do not be over-zealous in communications with festival organisers who, because of their workload, tend to communicate by blanket email when it comes to information on venues, green rooms, travel arrangements and reimbursement processes.

Do feel that you can send individual emails when you are invited to do so, or where you have a special requirement – such as one deriving from a disability – but don't send individual emails about information likely to be sent in circulars.

Once your booking has been confirmed, do not send further emails because you think you should have heard a response by a certain time. You are on the mailing list and will be told when organisers are ready to send information out. Dealing with super-fluous emails will only delay their schedule.

If there is a reason you need to know detailed information in advance, for example, if you need to book time off work to attend, state this clearly when confirming your acceptance, giving as much information as possible.

If the organiser has offered to sell your books in the festival bookstore, it is your responsibility to ensure that your books arrive in the right place at the right time, and that unsold books are collected promptly according to their requirements.

Be professional and organised. This doesn't just mean turning up when and where you are supposed to. It means anticipating any needs you may have and stating them clearly at the earliest possible opportunity.

Keep an up-to-date biography at all times, in various lengths that can be sent promptly, upon request, for use in promotional material. (having one in 30, 50, 100 and 200 words means you're ready for all requests).

By adhering to these guidelines, with mutual respect and under-standing, self-published authors and festival organisers can work together to the considerable benefits of all concerned – especially that important end-user, the book-buyer. Now we move on to another influential area that affects those buyer's perceptions of a book: the world of prizes and awards.

8. Awards & Prizes

THERE ARE A myriad of literary prizes for books in all genres and of all themes and backgrounds. Our focus in this section is on major prizes, in part because what is true in regard to dealing with them is equally true all the way down the ladder, and in part because many of the smaller prizes are already more flexible. What readers and writers need to see is an opening of the doors at the top, bringing self-publishing onto a wider platform. So our focus here is not on prizes open only to self-publishers. Again, there are many of these, some prestigious and increasingly high profile and undoubtedly there will be more in the coming years. Some, unfortunately, are mere money spinners for the organisers (see ALLi's Watchdog Page for more on this) but others do wonderful work that we wholeheartedly support. This book however, is about the opening of doors, about seeing all books included on the basis of content, regardless of their means of production, and so focusses on general prizes.

The experience of small, independent presses is in many ways an excellent illustration and template, both for self-publishing writers and for prize organisers. The 2012 Man-Booker Prize offers a fine illustration of the issues involved.

The prize attracted a lot of negative attention in 2011 following remarks by judges that they were looking for readable books. The shortlist of 2012 went a long way to silencing the critics, and the inclusion of books from small presses such as *The Lighthouse* (Salt) and *Swimming Home (And Other Stories)* were an important part of this. They made the case unequivocally for the literary quality of the output from small presses and for the centrality of small presses to the best of contemporary literature.

Small presses in general were being talked about in the papers as well as the individual books. It seems reasonable that all books, however they are produced, should be compared on an equal basis for what they say and how they say it, rather than how they came into being. If entry for most high profile and prestigious prizes is opened up to self-published alongside trade-published authors, the best writing will rise to the top, regardless of its origin – and it will soon be clear that self-published books can be of the very highest quality.

It is only when the major national and international awards are truly inclusive that good writing of all kinds may compete on an equal footing.

Why Book Awards Matter

Oscar Wilde had it right when he said comparisons are odious — and literary comparisons most odious of all. The best book award schemes, however, perform three important tasks:

- Recognise and validate excellence;

- Bring good books within a defined field to readers interested in that area; and

- Help talented writers build careers that enable them to write more.

Winning a major book award is a clear indicator to the book-buying public of a book's worth, at least as perceived by the judges of that prize. The power of a prize-winner's – even a shortlisted runner-up's - sticker on a book cover has power to boost sales, whether or not the books bought because of it are actually read and enjoyed by the general public, or left gathering dust on the coffee-table to impress visitors.

The top literary prizes are very high profile, making news headlines many times over each time they are awarded. Announcements of long-lists, shortlists, winners and the aftermath all provide valuable publicity for those authors lucky enough to be involved.

Many other benefits may be gained beyond the winner's cash prize – $10k for the Pulitzer, £50k for the Man Booker, and a staggering Swedish Kronor 8 million for the Nobel Prize for Literature. The winner may expect to accrue increased sales in the home market, new or extended contracts from overseas, sales of translation rights, higher advances for future commissions, and greater visibility for their backlist.

One might even go as far as to include ironic awards, such as the highly-regarded *Literary Review*'s infamous Bad Sex Awards, given to the most excruciating passage describing explicit sex. Even this kind of award can help an author to sell more books and raise their profile and any awards with any degree of marketing clout for any book may be covetable for an author.

With such massive prizes – and potential profits for publishers – it is no surprise that the top awards sometimes seem to be little short of a battleground for competing publisher armies. To say that the big trade publishers – and their authors – are keen to enter is an understatement. Some writers even demand that their publisher include in their contract an agreement to enter their books for major prizes, at the publisher's expense.

Considering that the current terms for entry to the Man Booker Prize include a commitment from each entrant's publisher to contribute up to £10,000 towards the scheme's publicity costs, this is no small undertaking. There are also other demands that would be beyond the reach of most self-funding, self-publishing authors operating as individuals. For example, the publisher of the winning book must agree to make available to the award body within ten days of winning 1,000 copies of the book, presumably for publicity purposes.

Even without such conditions, there is a clause that seems specifically designed to knock author-publishers out of the running, for no apparent reason other than a pre-formed bias against any potential wannabe:

"Rule 3(d) Self published books are not eligible where the author is the publisher or where a company has been specifically set up to publish that book."

This rule seems hardly necessary, and it would dignify the Man Booker Prize to remove it, for even if technically they are allowed to enter, few self-published authors could afford the risk that they might win!

As well as the many, and proliferating, awards open exclusively for self-published authors, there are also mainstream award programmes that offer prizes to self-published books within a segregated category. One such programme is the UK Festival of Romance Awards programme, which includes an Award for Best Author-Published Novel and a New Talent Award, which is open to books as yet unpublished. The small print confirms that its definition of "as yet unpublished" includes self-published books.

Many self-published authors would find this attitude offensive and demeaning. One can only hope that any books entered in that category will gradually reform the system from within, demonstrating indisputably to the judges that their standards are on a professional par with the books in the trade-published categories.

No self-published authors has yet been awarded any of "The Big Three" the Pulitzer, the Man Booker or been awarded the Nobel Prize for Literature, though one did come close. Way ahead of her time in the self-publishing revolution, Jill Paton Walsh made the shortlist of the then Booker Prize in 1994 with *Knowledge of Angels*. (Read her account of her achievement here in The Guardian.)

At that time, author-publishing was available only to a small minority with specialist knowledge. Now that the digital revolution has kicked in, it can only be a matter of time before another self-published author's book is long-listed, short-listed and declared the winner.

A Question of Attitude?

Perhaps one reason for the low number of self-published entries for such literary awards is that self-published authors are too quick to assume they are not eligible for the big prizes, or to aim their sights lower, at what they perceive to be more achievable goals: smaller, lesser-known and specialist prizes.

Jamaican author Ezekel Alan almost didn't enter his self-published debut novel *Disposable People* for the Commonwealth Book Prize 2013, for which he was named a Regional Winner.

My first novel was written almost as a process of catharsis or perhaps exorcism – getting rid of some old ghosts from the past. A major national newspaper back home thought of it differently, however, and gave it rave reviews. Then the person who edited the book, a Brit, pointed out to me that the Commonwealth Book Prize was now open to self-published novels. I had known of the Commonwealth Book Prize before, but never once thought that my act of exorcism would even remotely be worthy of consideration for that award. The novel was entered, and became the first self-published book to win a major international prize. The publicity which ensued was overwhelming.

Author Ezekel Alan

Irish children's author Benji Bennett, by contrast, is now taking such things in his stride, winning the Children's category of the National Irish Book Awards not once, but twice, most recently in 2013 for *When You Were Born*. Reporting the award on his Independent Publishing Magazine blog, Mick Rooney wrote:

Ireland's premier national book award is unusual in that unlike other prestigious book awards, it does not preclude self-published titles from being nominated – requiring only that a a title should be written by an Irish author, published within the year of the awards, and in print and available through Irish book wholesalers. Titles are nominated and voted on equally by a panel of book industry experts and public online voting ... This is actually Benji Bennett's second time to win the children's category award (first in 2009) having self-published seven books since 2008.

Mick Rooney (Read the full article on Bennett's win here.)

There are also many other prestigious book awards around the world, albeit with a smaller purse and a wider remit than the "big three". Unless there are rules specifically excluding them, self-publishing authors should feel free to enter their books, if they are confident that the award is appropriate to their work and that their book is of a suitable category and standard.

For some time to come, every such award won will be a victory not only for the author, but for the cause of self-published authors everywhere.

A New Model: The Folio Prize

While there are still some awards that openly exclude self-published authors, many more are now welcoming them, recognising that they are becoming an intrinsic part of modern literature. New awards are being set up to be categorically inclusive from their very beginning to all authors, no matter how they are published. One of these, operating in the UK, is the Folio Prize, sponsored by The Folio Society, a long-established publisher of luxury editions of classic and modern classic books — including, interestingly and fittingly, some titles that were originally self-published (by such luminaries as Virginia Woolf and Mark Twain).

Founded in 2013, The Folio Prize is especially inclusive because it allows for books that have been published in any format, print or digital, which clearly opens doors for the self-published on a budget. In so doing, they emphasise the most important quality of books: to connect with readers and, to quote the stated aim of the charity, "to bring great writing and an enthusiasm for reading to the public".Five members of The Folio Academy will consider 80 books, 60 of which will be nominated from within the Academy, but 20 more chosen from entries submitted by publishers — including self-publishers. From a shortlist of eight, the winner will emerge with a cash prize of £40k.

Only books published in the UK during the relevant qualifying year are eligible, but it is hoped that this model sets a precedent that will be followed elsewhere.

Prizes Exclusively for Self-Published Authors

Another interesting award the International Rubery Book Award, which is open only to self-published books or books from small independent presses, which it defines as any imprint not owned by the "Big Five" trade publishers — Penguin/Random House, Hachette, Harper Collins, Macmillan and Simon & Schuster.

There are many more self-published books prizes. It is really down to the individual author to seek out the awards that feel the best fit for their work in terms of territory, genre and attitude – and also to decide when it's better to walk away than to submit your book for an unworthy award.

Or to consider whether prizes are important at all. Many self-published authors feel that spending time seeking out such awards would be better spent writing and actively building a direct relationship with your reader community. Bestselling and acclaimed novelist, Linda Gillard, has this to say:

Having been shortlisted for/won various awards over the years I've never seen anything other than very short-term exposure & no sub-sequent improvement at all in sales. I really don't think readers care about awards or competitions. (Look at Fifty Shades) Have you ever bought a book because it won a comp? I haven't. I don't think anything sells books apart from readers talking positively about them and retailer promotions. So I'm always looking for what's quick to do, what's free.

I think there's something else to be said about competitions and prizes. You're almost setting yourself up to fail. Who needs that? We didn't become writers to win. I'm thinking of a friend of mine who won a prestigious BBC scriptwriting competition. She entered the following year & wasn't long-listed — well obviously. She'd won the year before! — but she beats herself up about not even being long-listed. She's the kind of writer where failure goes deep, but success is flukey.

If you're that sort of person, competitions can be a stick (and probably an expensive stick) to beat yourself with. I think it's like everything else we discuss at ALLi – if you enjoy it, do it, then let it go. It's the expectations that do the damage, in my opinion. And the sense of good writing time wasted.

Author Linda Gillard

How To Choose Awards To Enter

Clearly, it is down to the individual author to decide whether or not to submit their work for competitions. If you decide to give it a try, proceed with caution, or you may do more harm than good, both to your own reputation and to that of the self-publishing movement as a whole.

When you find an award that seems a good match for your work, don't rush in, but read the submission guidelines carefully and work out exactly how much it will cost you. This may be more than is immediately evident: as well as the entry fee, if you have to send a quantity of print books, include their cost and the price of shipping in your calculation.

For example, one well-known, online award programme specifically for self-published books requires a $75 fee per entry in a single category (add another $50 per additional category), plus the submission of two print books (for which add your shipping costs). There are 60 categories, and many books would fall into more than one. Although there are a handful of larger prizes, the first prize in each category is just $100, a medal, a certificate and a number of stickers for your books. How many stickers? Five! If you want more, you have to pay for them! Oh, and there's an invitation to attend an awards ceremony in New York. Doubtless, you will get a bill for that too.

Sadly, there appears to be no shortage of entrants. Many of the top prize winners have fewer than 20 reviews each on Amazon. com, some not flattering.

In the same vein that Michael N. Marcus declared on the ALLi blog that every book can now be a bestseller (read his entertaining post here), if put in a sufficiently rarefied category, doubtless every book can win a prize, provided you are prepared to pay for entry to enough indiscriminate award schemes.

The fact that awards charge for entry in itself should not deter. It is not unreasonable to ask entrants who are taking a small punt on winning to contribute to the considerable costs of running such a programme. After all, it is you, not the organisers of the award scheme, who will ultimately profit from increased sales if you win.

That is why many major award schemes can only operate by attracting commercial sponsors who invest in return for publicity for their own business.

However, before proceeding, ascertain whether the award programme you wish to enter is charging a reasonable and affordable fee, in relation to any benefits winning might yield. Are the costs balanced by the benefits?

If you think yes, then next examine their marketing material: their website, the awards they offer, their promotional activity. Does it look professional? An amateurish award logo won't do your book or your author website any favours; in fact, it does the opposite.

Finally, if they've passed these tests, take time to research previous winners. Have you heard of them? If not, look them up on Amazon. Take a "look inside" their books, read their reviews. Does what you see marry up with their status as an award-winning author? If not, it is reasonable to assume that the award is a scam to extract money from naïve newbie authors, so click away and move on.

In the greater scheme of the *Open Up To Indie Authors* campaign, applying for these awards is unlikely to help self-published authors gain equal recognition with trade-published, but will only serve to deepen the divide.

And ultimately, of course, the award that matters most of all is great feedback, unsolicited, from loyal readers. Certainly not paid-for endorsement by charlatans that no-one has ever heard of.

A Note re Quality Control Awards

Book awards that single out winners from the pack are not to be confused with the quality control awards offered by book evaluation sites such as Awesome Indies. These organisations judge books not against each other, but against professional standards of publication. For readers who are wary of self-published authors, these can provide useful reassurance, and also boost the confidence of the submitting author. At the same time, they draw attention to the fact that a book has been self-published. Their badge of approval can therefore be displayed on a book jacket not only as a sign that

the content is of a professional standard, but also as a proud asser-
tion of the author's self-published status.

Clearly, winning a mainstream award, or a valued award of any
kind, is a wonderful achievement for any self-published author.
Another establishment endorsement yet to be cracked is the admission of self-published authors to professional bodies for writers.
To this analogous situation we now turn.

9. Associations & Societies

JOINING A PROFESSIONAL organisation for writers can be as much an affirmation for some authors as seeing their name on the cover of their first book. Self-published authors of the joining kind are keen to become a member of whatever professional body is their natural home.

Such organisations are many and varied. These range from the catch-all Society of Authors in the UK, the The Writers' Guild or Career Writers' Association in the USA, or the Writers' Union of Canada, for example, to genre groups such as:

- Romance Writers of America (RWA), the Romantic Novelists' Association (RNA), *(Romance)*.

- Crime Writers Association (CWA), Mystery Writers of America (MWA), International Thriller Writers (ITW), Sisters In Crime (SIC). *(Thrillers)*

- The Historical Novelist's Society (HNS), *(Historical novels)*.

- The Society of Children's Book Writers and Illustrators (SCBWI), *(Children's)*.

- The Science Fiction and Fantasy Writers of America (SFWA), Broad Universe (BU), *(sci-fi and fantasy)*

Specialist groups united by something other than the content of their books may also gather together, like The Society of Women Writers and Journalists or the European Medical Writers Association.

Some authors join writers' organisations to share specific benefits offered by the group, which may be very wide indeed for those that are effectively trades unions. Others may join simply as a statement that they have arrived as a writer. It is down to the individual to choose how much they wish to engage with any such organisation. Some writers are simply not natural joiners of anything, and if that suits them best, that's fine. Others wish to play a full and active part, taking their place alongside trade-published authors for the greater good of all concerned.

Choosing The Best Association For You.

Biggest or longest established doesn't necessarily mean best, even though the larger the group, the more negotiating power it has to gain discounts and benefits for its members. Local chapters of big organisorganisationsorganisationations such as the RWA or HNS or small, local independent groups that are more accessible and personal may be more helpful to you in furthering your writing. Bristol Women Writers, which admits only ten authors at any time, and the South Carolina Writers' Workshop, are two names that cropped up during the research for this book.

Even the most ardent campaigner will understand that these professional bodies, many of them very long-established, are protective of their reputation and are nervous of devaluing membership by admitting authors who may bring the organisation into disrepute. All well and good – except when a self-published author wishes to join an association that vets applicants according to how their book has been published. Thus, two authors whose work is of equal quality and whose books, to the eye of the humble reader, look equally professional and appealing, will receive different treatment, because one has been published by a third party and the other has not.

Even worse is if such discrimination happens between authors where the self-published author's work is better written, more professionally produced, sells more copies, and is part of a more extensive oeuvre than is true of many trade-published authors.

What will it mean when a writer sells thousands of books but fails to secure a review or secret handshake from a union tribunal? That they're not really a professional writer? That they're not part of Canada's cultural landscape? I find that preposterous. And until the rules to join the union are the same for everyone, I'm just not interested.

*Debut novelist Maia Sepp (*see her guest post on the ALLi blog for her full argument*).*

Entry By Merit

Deciding on the basis of whether or not the author is self-published seems a rather blunt instrument, as readers buying ever-increasing numbers of self-published books. "Organisations should serve their members, says indie author Karen Myers. "Rigidity in the face of opportunity is not a useful solution for anyone."

A more rational approach would be to consider each applicant on the merits of their actual work, to be judged by the membership panel of the organisation concerned.

There are ways of doing this that would be open to public scrutiny, such as those used by some of the indie book evaluation sites – for example, average star rating on Amazon, or a minimum of top reviews – but such a system might be too open to manipulation or abuse, as well as giving more weight to Amazon reviewers than many authors and publishers would find palatable.

The number of copies sold might also be considered, but this approach does not compare like with like. Niche books for narrow interest groups seldom sell in great quantities, and the sales rank of books with high literary merit is likely to rank far below crass best-sellers shifting millions to the masses.

It would therefore seem more appropriate that applications for membership from self-published authors might include an examination of the actual book by the organisation's membership committee. (Even fairer if trade-published authors have to undergo the same treatment.) Applicants might be invited to submit a copy of each of their books with their membership form to facilitate inspection of their work with minimal administration or cost to the organisation. The basis of their decision would be private, but the panel's honesty would be taken on trust.

Already Opening Up – A Little

In time, too, there should be less need for such a time-consuming process, because a growing number of authors' associations are already opening up to indies, allowing self-published authors to join the fold.

However, some are doing so tentatively, and in ways that perpetuate discrimination, allowing self-published authors to join only as associates — in effect, second-class citizens who may not to enjoy full membership rights. Some indies view this as start in the right direction. Rather than reject such membership, they prefer to join in whatever way possible and try to influence the organisation's attitude from within. This allows them to get to know how the group operates and to understand its culture better than as a non-member on the outside, lobbying for equal rights.

Others view such tiered membership as a grudging insult added to the original injury and feel that joining on this basis would make them an enabler, allowing prejudice to continue.

I will not accept the role of a second-class citizen voluntarily, not as an indie writer, not as a female, not in any capacity. If the writer organisations get around to recognising a broader membership group, I may reconsider, but not unless there is no distinction based on indie/traditional.
Karen Myers.

Knocking at the Door

If there really are no options to join your preferred organisation as a self-published author, it is worth writing a considered, courteous letter to express your reasons for wanting to join, your track record as a self-published author, and enclosing the sample of your work that is most likely to demonstrate that you would be a worthy member. Sending them an impressive book of professional quality will be the most persuasive action, or you might consider the kind of query letter normally sent to an agent or publisher, including a short extract, brief and easy to read.

This may help to open the door of resistance that first important chink, especially if many excellent self-published authors do the same. If they still refuse, a courteous reply stating your disappointment, and expressing a continuing interest should they change their policy in future, will keep all parties' options open.

Alternatively, you may decide to switch. Best-selling novelist Linda Gillard, both trade- and self-published, says: "After many years' membership, I have not renewed at the Society of Authors this year. I decided they weren't offering me anything that ALLi wasn't offering."

ALLi: The Alliance of Independent Authors.

Now, thanks to founding director Orna Ross, recently named by The Bookseller magazine (the bible of the British book trade) as "one of the 100 most influential people in publishing", there is one thriving organisation that all self-published authors may join: The Alliance of Independent Authors, fondly known as ALLi (to rhyme with "ally").

An Inclusive Association

ALLi members include many of the most experienced and successful self-publishing authors in existence, but newcomers and aspiring self-publishers are warmly welcomed. Some members have also been trade-published, and some have worked in related industries such as marketing and promotion. They are a smart, knowledgeable, well-connected group – and, as professional writers, well placed to tell their story and campaign for equal rights for indies.

So that ALLi is open to all, membership fees are kept as affordable possible, made possible by subsidies from large players in the associated services (Amazon, Kobo and Ingram), and ALLi has negotiated many attractive discounts which, for some members, may entirely offset the cost of their annual subscription.

ALLi is open not just to authors who are exclusively self-published, but also to those who, like its founder, have come from a trade publishing background or who earn a publishing contract as a result of successful self-publishing. No stigma is attached to any author's choice, and all pathways to publication are respected.

- Authors who make their living from self-publishing and associated work such as teaching or lecturing may opt for Professional membership.

- Organisations or individuals who offer high quality services for self-published authors are welcome as Partner members.

- Those who have not yet self-published a book but aspire to do so are welcome to join as Associate members, upgrading to Author status on publication.

A Sharing Association

ALLi shares its members' knowledge and debate far beyond the bounds of its membership. It maintains an authoritative blog of self-publishing advice as a service to the community and its guidebooks, free to members, are available for non-members to buy.

ALLi members may also talk in confidence via private groups such as its lively Facebook forum. A member may ask a question about any aspect of self-publishing in the knowledge that helpful replies will be posted by those who have experienced and resolved the same issue. The collegiate, democratic and supportive spirit is enjoyed by all.

All genres of fiction, nonfiction and poetry are represented within ALLi's membership, and all ranges of ambition. While many authors seek and find commercial success and profit with books of popular appeal to the mass market, ALLi's membership reaches far beyond the strictly commercial aims associated with trade publishing houses. There are experimental authors, literary writers and creative mavericks for whom commercial viability is irrelevant or even undesirable.

ALLi's self-published authors may be very individual, but they are increasingly professional and successful, winning prestigious awards, hitting bestseller lists and being offered (and often rejecting) trade publishing contracts.

A Caring Association

ALLi is now a force to be reckoned with: it has become the reference source of choice for the media on self-publishing issues. Its founder, advisory panel and members are increasingly invited to write and speak about self-publishing in the press and on national and international TV. This collection of endorsements of ALLi by its members in the blog post "Why I'm A Member of the Alliance of Independent Authors", summarises some of the many benefits of membership — as perceived by the members themselves.

ALLi is also very caring of its members, offering them a dedicated, determined Watchdog service to root out and expose unscrupulous service providers, guarding self-published authors everywhere against exploitation. There are still plenty of organisations out there who see would-be self-published authors as easy prey. Sometimes, and surprisingly to those not in the know, these can even be subsidiaries of trade publishing houses. Writers already in the clutches of charlatans will, on approaching ALLi, be helped to extract themselves and find better alternatives. This is extremely important work.

The ALLi Watchdog team also issues regular warnings on the blog and have compiled a regularly updated, comprehensive handbook, *Choosing A Self-Publishing Service*, (free to ALLi members), which details how to use such services effectively and includes warnings against the pitfalls to avoid. This publication is available for purchase by non-members.

One sign of its success and impact is that its membership reaches beyond authors who are solely self-published. There are plenty of hybrid authors and ex-trade-turned-self-published authors who have applied to join, to mark their support for its work, such as the best-selling, highly respected Susan Hill, who has been quietly self-publishing in tandem with her trade-published success and very much enjoying the benefits.

ALLi will continue to welcome all authors who are interested in self-publishing to its mutually supportive community.

Equal Pay for Equal Work

Regardless of which organisations self-published authors may choose or be allowed to join, another area in which equal rights are sought is in remuneration for work provided. Clearly, self-published authors make their own marketing judgments and decisions when setting the prices for their books, but many members of ALLi also produce or contribute to newspapers, magazines, journals, newsletters, pamphlets and trade-published books, published by small and large presses with local, national or international distribution. Some also write for screen, stage, radio, apps or websites, and engage in public speaking at conferences and other events. All of these activities will command fees set by third parties, and we have already touched on the tricky subject of gaining fair remuneration for such work in the previous Chapter on Festivals. Theoretically, rates of pay should take into account the time and effort members devote to researching as well as writing and/or speaking when making public appearances. Out-of-pocket expenses incurred for such engagements such as travel, accommodation and subsistence should be reimbursed for authors of any kind.

It is not in ALLi's remit to produce an exhaustive and universally applicable guide to rates and conditions for writers across such a broad spectrum of activities, territories and regions – nor would it be easy to do so. However, any self-published authors who are engaged in such work are advised to seek equivalent treatment to their trade-published peers. One important part of the *Open Up To Indie Authors* campaign is to work towards uniformity of practices in the literary, academic and publishing workspaces. If you are unsure of the appropriate rate for a piece of work, consult your local author societies, unions and guilds and, wherever possible, stand your ground to negotiate appropriate fees.

Please feel free to contact ALLi if you need further support or guidance.

PART THREE

Towards An Open Future

10. Opening Up

WHATEVER LIES AHEAD for the book trade as it continues to evolve at high speed and in tandem with technological advances and innovations, one thing is certain: self-published authors are here to stay, championed by the Alliance of Independent Authors (ALLi), and all who support them within and outside the author community.

In this book we have addressed the most important areas in which self-published authors seek recognition on an equal footing with their trade-published peers. We hope that the candid and constructive overview offered by this book will encourage all parties discussed to work together for their mutual benefit.

Aside from the key areas covered in previous chapters in which more work is needed to open up the way for all authors to be treated equally, there are many other avenues by which all self-published authors may actively demonstrate the quality of their books to the public at large.

Every self-published author is an ambassador for the *Open Up To Indie Authors* campaign, and no self-published author is an island. If you are a writer, remember that every piece of marketing activity you undertake not only helps sell your books but also furthers the cause of the self-publishing sector as a whole. Every new reader won over, every good book sold, helps persuade the reading public, and the old guard of the publishing establishment, of the quality and value of self-published work. All writers have a responsibility to our readers to make our books the best they can be before publication.

Then we can stand up, be counted and wear our self-published author badge with pride – one of the growing numbers of writers whose books are as enticing and satisfying as those emerging from trade-press publications. Nothing will be more powerful than our own pro-active involvement in moving the self-publishing community forward on the road to equal opportunities.

Share your achievement wherever you can, online and offline. Engage with your local media and reach out to books groups. Connect with your neighbourhood libraries and bookstores and festivals. Reach out further via free book missions: BookCrossing, Books on the Underground and Books on the Subway. Seek new and creative methods of writing, publishing and promotion. Aim high and help each other.

Whether you are an author, a librarian, a reviewer, a festival organiser, a bookstore owner, or have some other role within the book trade and its associated businesses and nonprofits, please join in and spread the word about our great movement, however you can. Writing, publishing, reaching readers: these are important jobs with a great deal of influence in society. Wherever we are placed within those sectors, we all share a common bond: the desire to bring great books to readers, who will be the ultimate judges of our work and its merit.

Please sign the Open Up To Indies Petition

We warmly invite you to sign our petition to help us further the Open Up To Indies campaign. You can do so here: https://www.change.org/en-GB/petitions/open-up-to-indie-authors/.

Feedback Welcome

We also welcome any comments, clarifications, updates, or additions to any section of this book, so that we may update it regularly and keep it representative the current state of the industry. You can contact us any time through our contact form on the ALLi website.

And Finally...

To close on a light and up-to-the-minute note, here's one indication of the ever-strengthening foothold of self-publishing within the book trade. In the new re-make of the long-running television series, *Murder, She Wrote*, the amateur sleuth heroine will be not a trade-published writer, like the original Jessica Fletcher, played so memorably by Angela Lansbury, but an author who has just self-published her debut novel. We're hoping she's signed our petition...

Appendix One:
ALLi Code for Author Collaborations

Festivals

As a writer looking to speak at your festival, I undertake:

- To provide information, pictures, promotional details in a timely fashion

- To be professional in requesting technical/digital equipment well in advance, and providing powerpoint slides and handouts in advance

- To be punctual and prompt in arriving at the festival, at the green room, and at the event venue

- To prepare travel claims and invoices in a professional, timely fashion

- To liaise with festival bookshops and make books available in advance as required

Reviewers

In return for having my book reviewed on your blog/publication I undertake:

- To make my book available to you in your preferred format

- To respond informatively and in timely manner to readers' questions, should that be your blog policy

- Not to respond negatively to your comments, or to those of your readers

- Not to respond at all, should that be your blog's policy

- To use all my social media contacts to promote your blog. This consists of: (list twitter followers, Facebook likes, length of email list, blog followers etc.)

Bookstores

In return for having my book stocked in your store, I undertake:

- To make my books available to you in your preferred ordering fashion

- To collect all unsold books within one week of receiving notice from you should you wish to take books in person on consignment

- To otherwise to ensure that a full returns service is in operation

- To list your store on my website as a stockist of my book

- To encourage readers wishing to purchase physical copies of my book to do so through their local bookshop

- To sign copies in store should you wish

- To run an event of your choosing

- To ensure that my book is available in your preferred sizing

Libraries

In return for having my book stocked in your library, I undertake:

- To make my books available to you in your preferred ordering fashion

- To list your library on my website as a stockist of my book

- To encourage local readers to borrow the book and comment on your website

- To run an event of your choosing

- To donate as many copies of my book as you require in your preferred sizing and format

Appendix Two:
Note re Terms of Reference

Approach any ten people on the street and ask them to define self-publishing, and you are likely to receive ten different answers. As self-publishing evolves, its terms of reference are rapidly changing.

Many authors who publish their own work are uncomfortable with the term "self-published", which gives the impression that they have done absolutely everything required to produce the book themselves, from cover design to editing. This is misleading. Good author publishing requires running a team of specialist services. New, more accurate, terms are becoming more common but have not yet taken precedence in search engines over the catch-all term "self-publishing".

The Alliance of Independent Authors (ALLi) uses the following terms of reference, which are also used throughout this book:

Author: A published writer — the word comes from the Latin verb *augere*, "to make grow, to originate".

Self-published author: any author who has published a book at personal expense. Self-publishers range the full gamut, from those publishing a one-off book for family and friends to the most entrepreneurial and productive author-publisher.

Author-publisher: Authors who make a living from writing and publishing their own books. Those primarily motivated by commercial success are sometimes called authorpreneurs; those primarily motivated by creative concerns are often overlooked but exist in increasing numbers. The Alliance of Independent Authors has a professional membership category for such writers.

Trade publisher: Businesses that licence publishing rights from authors and handle the publication of their books in return for a large percentage. (Also sometimes called "legacy" or "traditional" publishing). Most of trade publishing is handled by what are known as The Big Five: Penguin-Random House; Hachette Book Group (HBG); Harper Collins, Macmillan and Simon & Schuster.

Independent or "indie" press or publisher: A small publishing company which, like the big conglomerates, commissions books from authors and publishes at the company's expense, not the author's. (May or may not be run by authors who also use the firm to self-publish).

Publishing Service: A service used by an author to help them to publish their book. Can be freelance one-person operations, like designers or editors, to full-scale services including editorial, design and marketing which get paid upfront. Payment to services can take three forms: upfront payment; royalty split or percentage payment; licensing to trade publishers in return for small royalty and advance. Also called **Author Services**.

All of these terms are of little significance to our average reader, who simply wants a good book, professionally produced. In time, we will all just be authors, working on a level playing field, with equal opportunities. This guide has been devised to help hasten the arrival of that day.

About The Authors

Dan Holloway

I started my self-publishing journey on January 2nd 2009 when I posted a manifesto on Myspace entitled "Let's Make 2009 Publishing's Year Zero." Within a week or so, 22 writers from 8 countries had got together to form Year Zero Writers, a collective of self-publishing literary and experimental fiction writers who were frustrated with the increasingly narrow mainstream staple of traditional publishing. We were very lucky. We made a lot of noise and because the playing field was relatively clear at that point, people let us have our say. Within a year, I had written pieces about self-publishing for half the internet, was listed as one of Mashable's top writers on twitter (the first time, incidentally, I appeared alongside Orna), had my debut novel listed as one of *ebooksjustpublished*'s top 10 DRM-free books of 2009, and had launched Year Zero Writers live at the iconic Rough Trade on Brick Lane.

It's been a bit of a whirl since then. I have built on the relationships established with live venues in those early days, appearing at Stoke Newington Literary Festival for the past three years, coordinating the poetry for Chipping Norton Literary Festival, performing at Cheltenham Poetry Festival and Brighton Fringe, and winning the international spoken word show Literary Death Match as the only self-published author taking part. And I›ve been lucky enough to get articles about self-publishing into the national press. There is a world of wonderful opportunities out there for the self-published author. But for most of us, most of the time, those opportunities have to be harder fought for, and that›s why a book like this matters so much. www.eightcuts.com

Debbie Young

Like Alice down the rabbit-hole, I fell into self-publishing more or less by accident. Persuaded to trade for a more practical career my childhood ambition to become an author, I spent the next couple of decades applying my writing skills to the commercial world. Whether working in journalism, public relations or marketing, my brief was always to build understanding between my employers and their target audiences.

A significant birthday provided the wake-up call – or perhaps the excuse - to dredge back up my youthful ambition. When I went freelance in 2010, a chance conversation resulted in my first book commission. While researching "Sell Your Books!" for author-services provider, SilverWood Books, I realised for the first time the enormity of the self-publishing revolution, and I wanted to be a part of it.

Having joined ALLi almost as soon as it was formed, I welcomed Orna's invitation in 2013 to become Editor of its Self-Publishing Advice blog. I've now evolved into an ambassador and evangelist for the movement, speaking at public events and writing for other publications to raise awareness of the opportunities that self-publishing offers to aspiring and established authors alike.

As co-author of *Opening Up To Indie Authors*, I've found enormous satisfaction in deploying the skills and experience gained in my previous career for the good of the self-publishing movement. I hope and believe that this book will foster better understanding and cooperation between indie authors and all sectors of the publishing trade — and decimate misplaced resentment, helping to shape a brighter future for us all. www.authordebbieyoung.com

Orna Ross (Series Editor)

Orna Ross worked for 20 years in media and publishing, and published fiction and non-fiction with both small and corporate publishing houses before striking out on her own in 2011. The experience of publishing her own work, which she describes as "radically empowering", led her to form The Alliance of Independent Authors in 2012. Orna writes and publishes novels, poems and nonfiction about the creative process and has been named "One of the 100 Most Influential People in Publishing" (The Bookseller). When she's not writing or publishing, you'll probably find her reading. www.ornaross.com.

More ALLi Guidebooks

The Alliance of Independent Authors publishes a growing library of industry guides for self-publishing writers, drawing on the wisdom and experiences of its advisor and member network.

Choosing A Self-Publishing Service 2015. Jim Giammetteo

(Publication Autumn 2014)

How to find the ideal self-publishing service, whether you're in search of a freelance editor or designer or seeking a full-range assisted publisher. Includes a listing of Alliance of Independent Authors Partner Members, who provide vetted and approved services.

How To Self-Publish & Sell Your Book. Debbie Young & Catriona Troth

(Publication Autumn 2014).

A basic self-publishing primer backed by information and examples from The Self-publishing Advice Blog.

How I Do It: Tips From Successful Self-Publishers. Debbie Young (editor)

(Publication Spring 2015.)

Interviews with successful indie authors from The Self-Publishing Advice Blog.

How Authors Sell Rights.
Orna Ross & Danny McKerchar.

(Publication Autumn 2015)

Being a successful indie author means understanding that you sell not just books but publishing rights. This guide draws together advice from a number of sources to explain such rights in clear language, without legal jargon, from the author's perspective. Full of advice on how to best sell rights in the new publishing landscape and ensure you get a good deal. Includes examples of good contracts and negotiating tips.

The Alliance of Independent Authors (ALLi)

is a nonprofit, professional association for self-publishing writers.
www.allianceindependentauthors.org

BLOG: Enjoy special offers, signed books,
audio readings & free giveaways at:

www.selfpublishingadvice.org

Reviews on this book's Amazon, Goodreads or Kobo pages are
welcome and very much appreciated.

34913280R00075

Made in the USA
Charleston, SC
22 October 2014